The Kugaluk Site and the Nuvorugmiut

The Archaeology and History of a Nineteenth-Century Mackenzie Inuit Society

David A. Morrison

Canadian Museum of Civilization
National Museums of Canada

Canadian Cataloguing in Publication Data

Morrison, David A.
   The Kugaluk site and the Nuvorugmiut: the archaeology and history of a nineteenth-century Mackenzie Inuit society

(Mercury series, ISSN 0316-1854)
(Paper/Archaeological Survey of Canada, ISSN 0317-2244; no. 137)
Includes abstract in French.
Bibliography: p.
ISBN 0-660-10778-3

1. Kugaluk Site (N.W.T.). 2. Inuit—Northwest Territories—Antiquities.* 3. Northwest Territories—Antiquities. 4. Inuit—Northwest Territories—History—19th century.* 5. Excavations (Archaeology)—Northwest Territories.
I. Canadian Museum of Civilization. II. Archaeological Survey of Canada. III. Title. IV. Series. V. Series: Paper (Archaeological Survey of Canada); no. 137.

E99 E7 M67 1988   971.9'20049   C88-099101-1

Printed and bound in Canada

Published by
Canadian Museum of Civilization
National Museums of Canada
Hull, Quebec
K1A 0M8

ASC Papers Coordinator
Richard E. Morlan

OBJECT OF THE MERCURY SERIES

The Mercury Series is designed to permit the rapid dissemination of information pertaining to the disciplines in which the Canadian Museum of Civilization is active. Considered an important reference by the scientific community, the Mercury Series comprises over three hundred specialized publications on Canada's history and prehistory.

Because of its specialized audience, the series consists largely of monographs published in the language of the author.

In the interest of making information available quickly, normal production procedures have been abbreviated. As a result, grammatical and typographical errors may occur. Your indulgence is requested.

Titles in the Mercury Series can be obtained by writing to the

   Mail Order Services
   Publishing Division
   Canadian Museum of Civilization
   Hull, Quebec
   K1A 0M8

   (613) 957-9905

BUT DE LA COLLECTION MERCURE

La collection Mercure vise à diffuser rapidement le résultat de travaux dans les disciplines qui relèvent des sphères d'activités du Musée canadien des civilisations. Considérée comme un apport important dans la communauté scientifique, la collection Mercure présente plus de trois cents publications spécialisées portant sur l'héritage canadien préhistorique et historique.

Comme la collection s'adresse à un public spécialisé celle-ci est constituée essentiellement de monographies publiées dans la langue des auteurs.

Pour assurer la prompte distribution des exemplaires imprimés, les étapes de l'édition ont été abrégées. En conséquence, certaines coquilles ou fautes de grammaire peuvent subsister : c'est pourquoi nous réclamons votre indulgence.

Vous pouvez vous procurer la liste des titres parus dans la collection Mercure en écrivant au :

   Service des commandes postales
   Division de l'édition
   Musée canadien des civilisations
   Hull (Québec)
   K1A 0M8

   (613) 957-9905

Abstract

Kugaluk (NgTi-1) is a small historic Inuit site located near the outlet of the Eskimo Lakes, in the western Canadian Arctic. From its location, it can be attributed to the Nuvorugmiut, one of the five branches or "societies" which comprised the historic Mackenzie Inuit. At contact the largest Inuit group in the Canadian Arctic, the culture and society of the Mackenzie Inuit was almost entirely obliterated over the course of the last century. Poorly distinguished from their neighbours and remote from trading posts on the Peel and Anderson rivers, the Nuvorugmiut receive only scant attention in contemporaneous historic accounts, and in retrospective testimony gathered by Stefansson (1914). What information is available suggests that they engaged in the summer-time hunting of bowhead whales as late as the 1880s, while later accounts focus on intensive caribou hunting at this time of year.

The Kugaluk site comprises three semi-subterranean houses and several outside activity areas, including tool-manufacturing localities, hearths, and a collapsed stage or meat rack. One house was excavated with its adjacent midden, along with the activity areas. A sample of over 45,000 animal bones was collected, and about 1000 artifacts were unearthed. Trade goods and other artifacts present at the site indicate an occupation date between about 1850 and 1875, most probably about 1860. The animal bone proved to be dominated by the remains of caribou, with at least 109 individual animals represented. The analysis of dental eruption patterns and of annular deposition lines in the cementum of caribou teeth suggest a multi-seasonal occupation centered around the August caribou migration.

The excavation and analysis of the Kugaluk site material greatly expands our present understanding of the Nuvorugmiut, and by extension the Mackenzie Inuit in general. Evidently, intensive summer caribou hunting was an important subsistence strategy even in the early contact period, and probably aboriginally as well. Apparently not all Nuvorugmiut followed the same subsistence round, especially during August, when there was a direct

iii

scheduling conflict between caribou hunting and bowhead whaling. It is suggested that the Nuvorugmiut, like other Western Eskimo, may have been a ranked or even stratified society, and that pronounced status differences may have accompanied different subsistence choices.

Résumé

Kugaluk (NgTi-1) est un petit site inuit de l'époque historique situé près de l'embouchure des lacs Eskimo, dans l'ouest de l'Arctique canadien. D'après son emplacement, on peut l'attribuer aux Nuvorugmiut, une des cinq branches ou <<sociétés>> qui constituaient les Inuit du Mackenzie. A l'époque des premiers contacts, ce groupe était le plus important groupe inuit de l'Arctique canadien, mais la culture et l'organisation de la société des Inuit du Mackenzie furent presque entièrement annihilées au cours du siècle dernier. Les Nuvorugmiut, difficilement distingués de leurs voisins et éloignés des postes de traite des rivières Peel et Anderson, sont à peine mentionnés dans les récits de l'époque et dans les témoignages rétrospectifs recueillis par Stefansson (1914). Les données que nous possédons donnent à croire qu'ils chassèrent la baleine boréale l'été jusqu'aux années 1880; des récits ultérieurs font état d'une chasse intensive au caribou à cette même époque de l'année.

Le site de Kugaluk comprend trois maisons semi-souterraines et plusieurs aires d'activité extérieures, notamment des endroits où l'on fabriquait des outils, des foyers et un échafaudage ou un treillage à viande écroulé. Une maison a été complètement fouillée ainsi que son dépotoir et des aires d'activité extérieures. On a recueilli plus de 45000 os d'animaux et mis au jour plus de 1000 objets. Les biens de troc et autres objets présents sur le site indiquent que celui-ci fut occupé entre 1850 et 1875, tout probablement vers 1860. On trouve surtout des os de caribou (au moins 109 individus). L'analyse de l'éruption des dents et des lignes de dépôt annulaires dans le cément des dents de caribou suggère une occupation multi-saisonnière centrée sur la migration des caribou, en août.

Les fouilles du site de Kugaluk et l'analyse de ce qui y a été exhumé ont permis d'accroître considérablement nos connaissances sur les Nuvorugmiut, et donc sur les Inuit du Mackenzie en général. Évidemment, la chasse intensive au caribou l'été était importante pour la subsistance

de ces populations même à l'époque des premiers contacts, et sans doute
aussi antérieurement. Les Nuvorugmiut n'adoptaient apparemment pas tous
le même mode de subsistance, en particulier en août où il y avait un
conflit entre les périodes de chasse au caribou et de chasse à la baleine
boréale. Il semble que la société des Nuvorugmiut, comme celle d'autres
Esquimaux de l'Ouest, était hiérarchisée ou même stratifiée, et que le
statut social des individus pouvait fort bien dépendre des modes de
subsistance choisis.

ACKNOWLEDGEMENTS

I would like to express my gratitude to a great many people who assisted in the Kugaluk site excavation and analysis. My wife, Mary Jo Morrison, found the site during a helicopter survey we did in 1984, and joined me and Ken Swayze (Simon Fraser University) for the 1985 excavation season. In 1986 my field crew consisted of Ken Swayze and two residents of Tuktoyaktuk; Alphonse Voudrach and Jack Noksana. Alphonse is a life-long resident of the Kugaluk area, and was an invaluable source of information on local conditions and recent history. He, of course, had long known of the existence of the site. Mr. Swayze is a long-time colleague in northern field work, and his hard work and initiative are much appreciated.

Faunal analysis was a long and exhaustive process, and I was assisted by several people, including Ellen Foulkes and Chris Monohan, who worked on the bird bones, and Arien Burke, who identified the screened fish bones. Steve Cumbaa and Darlene Balkwell of the Zooarchaeological Identification Centre, National Museum of Natural Sciences, also provided valuable information on faunal identifications. Graphs, maps and drawings were all produced by Dave Laverie, while Sterling Presley did the thin-sectioning and helped with the interpretation of annular lines in the caribou teeth. Karlis Karklin (Parks Canada) helped sort the glass beads and offered advice on their interpretation, while John Light and Douglas Bryce from Parks Canada offered similar help with the metal artifacts. Charles Hett and his crew at the Conservation Services Division of the Canadian Museum of Civilization performed the necessary treatments to preserve the metal and wooden artifacts.

Finally, I wish to thank Mary Jo Morrison, Richard Morlan and Robert McGhee for their editorial advice, and the Hamlet of Tuktoyaktuk, for its forbearance. Funds for this project were provided by the Archaeological Survey of Canada (Canadian Museum of Civilization), and by the Northern Oil and Gas Action Plan (NOGAP), while logistic support and helicopter transportation in the field was generously provided by the Polar Continental Shelf Project from their base at Tuktoyaktuk.

TABLE OF CONTENTS

List of Figures

List of Tables

List of Plates

CHAPTER ONE

THE NUVORUGMIUT

Introduction

The Kugaluk is a small river flowing into an estuary at the bottom of Liverpool Bay, east of Tuktoyaktuk, in the western Canadian Arctic. To the northwest a series of ice-push ridges known locally as the "the Fingers" provide the entrance into the Eskimo Lakes (actually a deep bay of the ocean), while to the north and east is the body of Liverpool Bay, and the Beaufort Sea beyond. The Kugaluk archaeological site (NgTi-1) is located on an island about 60 hectares in extent, one of many generally flat, deltaic islands in the southern portion of the estuary (Fig. 1). The southern half of this island is very low and flat, and floods at each high tide (tides in the area average about 60 or 70 cm). The northern half is several metres higher. Joining the two is a grassy bank about two metres high, and it is along the top of this bank that three semi-subterranean houses were erected sometime around the middle of the last century.

Contact History

The people who built these houses were, in all probability, members of a Mackenzie Inuit (Eskimo) group known as the Nuvorugmiut, or "people of Nuvurak". In the nineteenth century, Nuvurak was an important village on the northern coast of the Tuktoyaktuk Peninsula. According to testimony gathered early in this century (Stefansson 1914), it was the focal point of a territorial group, or "society" (Burch 1980), which may have numbered between 300 and 500 people at contact. The Mackenzie Inuit were divided into at least five such groups, stretching from the Alaska border to Cape Bathurst. The Nuvorugmiut were the second most easterly, bounded to the east by the Avvaqmiut of the Anderson River/Cape Bathurst area, and to the west by the Kittegaryumiut of the East Channel/Eskimo Lakes (Fig. 2). The territory of the Nuvorugmiut was centred on the Tuktoyaktuk Peninsula (see McGhee 1974: Map 2) but extended, evidently, south of the Fingers at least as far as the bottom of the Kugaluk estuary (see Stefansson 1914: 14, 355-356; Nuligak 1966: 72). The history and society of these people is poorly

FIGURE 1

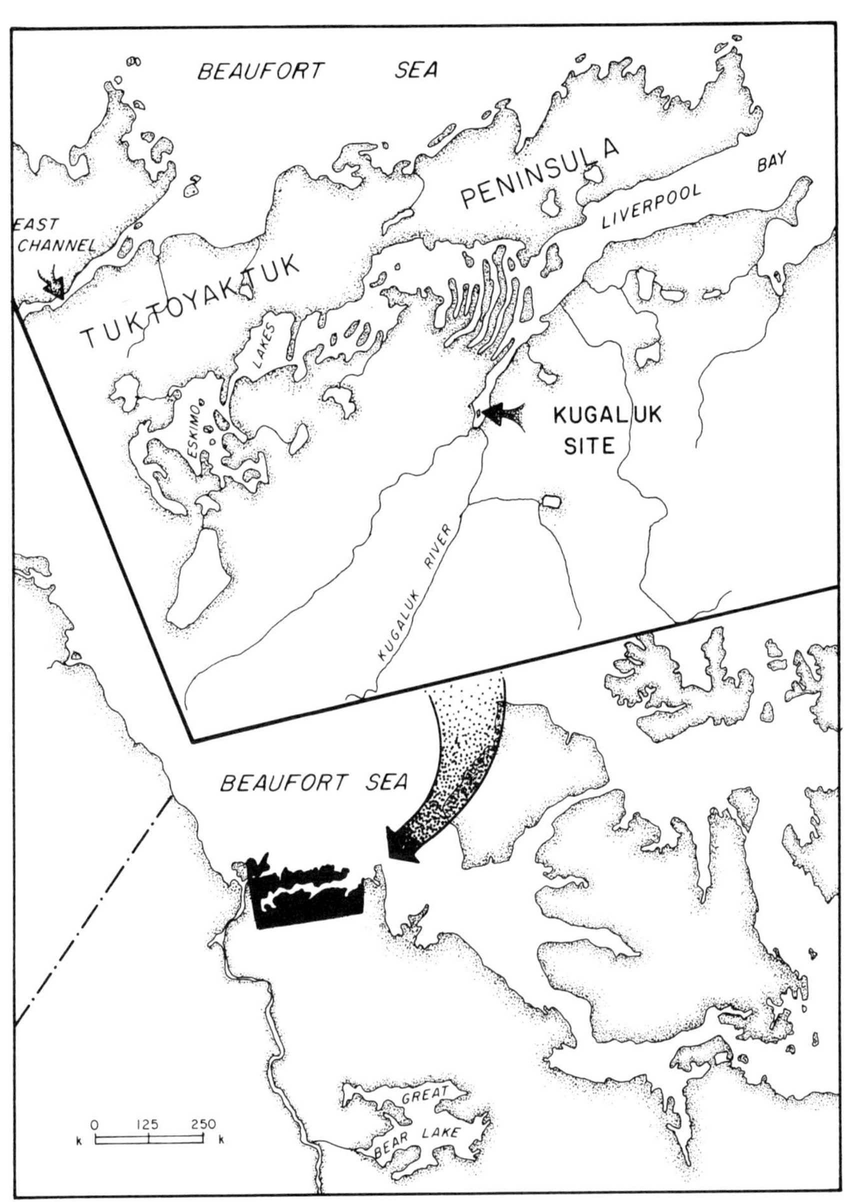

LOCATION OF THE KUGALUK SITE

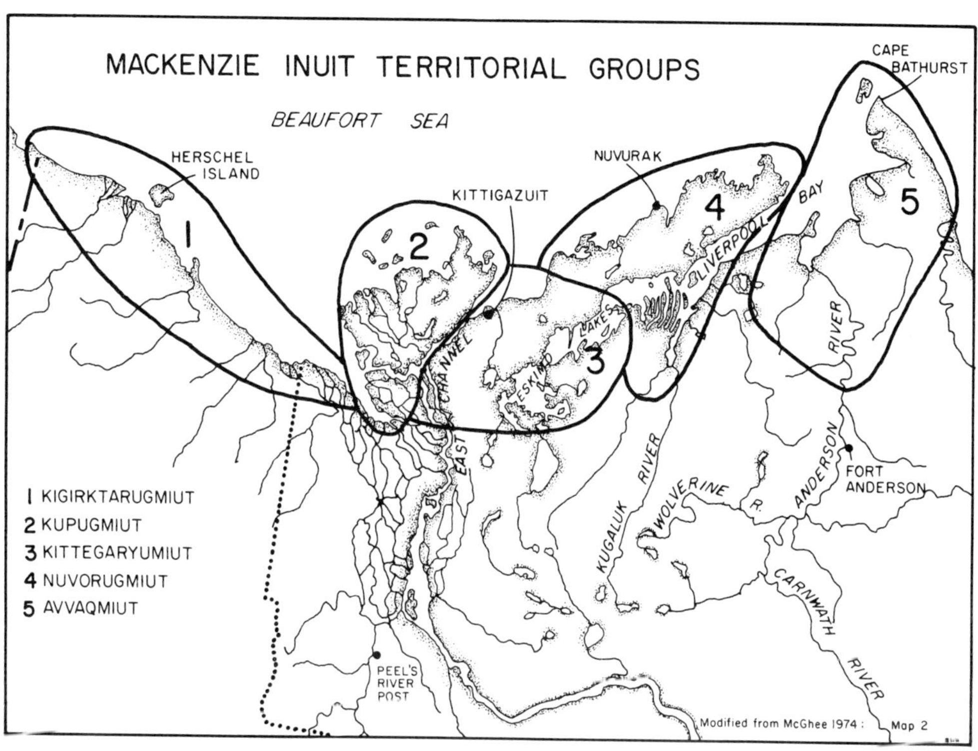

enough known to warrant a fairly detailed outline of the available
information, before turning our attention to the archaeology.

At contact the Mackenzie Inuit were the largest and richest Inuit
group in Canada, numbering between 2500 and 4000 people (Stefansson 1913:
452; Usher 1971: 171; McGhee 1974: 7). This was about equal to the total
Inuit population in the rest of Arctic Canada as far east as Hudson Bay.
Culturally they were quite distinct from the Central Eskimo to the east,
living for most of the winter in permanent driftwood houses rather than the
characteristic snowhouse. Indeed, their closest cultural affinities were with
Inupiat (Eskimo) groups living in north and west Alaskan, with whom they

had extensive trading relations. As Petitot (1970: 215) observed in the 1860s "our Eskimos always strive to imitate their western cousins. To them Eskimos from the east and from the north are outright savages."

This comparatively sophisticated and powerful culture was entirely destroyed over the course of the nineteenth century, the result of contact with, first, the Hudson's Bay Company and, second, the American Beaufort Sea whaling fleet. As is so often the case in Canadian history, it was a process initiated by the British, and completed by the Americans.

The first glimmer of contact with the outside world began for the Nuvorugmiut sometime in the late eighteenth century, as it did for the Mackenzie Inuit generally. Russian trade goods, principally iron and blue beads, had reached the Mackenzie Delta region via Alaskan Inupiat intermediaries at least as early as 1789 (Mackenzie 1970: 208; Franklin 1971: 130). This trade eventually penetrated as far east as Nuvurak and the Anderson River, and it was not until the late 1850s or early 1860s that competition with the Hudson's Bay Company brought it to an end (Richardson 1851: 354; HBC, B/6/a/1: 4).

The first direct contact between Mackenzie Inuit and Europeans occurred in 1799, when a party led by a Northwest Company trader named Livingstone was killed to a man somewhere along the East Channel (Wentzel 1823). In 1826 the Royal Navy sent the Second Franklin Expedition through the area in two parties (Franklin 1971). One was led by Franklin himself, and travelled down the West Channel and then along the Yukon Arctic coast to Alaska. The second party was under the command of Dr. John Richardson, who travelled down the East Channel, and then east along the Arctic Coast to Coronation Gulf. He was the first to visit the Nuvorugmiut on their home ground, arriving at the village of Nuvurak on July 13, 1826 (Franklin 1971: 215-217). He describes a village of 17 winter houses, and supplies a floor plan of "one of the largest". It is a cruciform structure similar to those known from elsewhere in the Mackenzie Inuit area (Petitot 1970: Fig. 29; Whittaker 1937: Fig. 7), with alcoves to accommodate four nuclear families. He also describes a "large building" or "assembly-room" which was 27 feet square on the inside, with the skulls of 21 bowhead whales around its base. "The general attention to comfort in the construction of the village, and the erection of a building of such

Richardson's view of Nuvurak in 1826 (re-drawn from Franklin 1971: Pl. 23). Note how the various buildings are made to resemble European houses.

magnitude, requiring an union of purpose in a considerable number of people, are evidences of no small progress towards civilization" (Richardson, in Franklin 1971: 217).

By the 1820s a second indirect source of European trade goods had opened up. Previously, Dene Indians (Loucheux and Hare) of the lower Mackenzie had received iron and other trade goods from the Mackenzie Inuit (Mackenzie 1970: 192; Simpson 1843: 103). However, by at least the 1820s they were themselves in direct contact with the Hudson's Bay Company at Fort Good Hope, and as the direction of trade reversed, actively assumed the role of middlemen (Franklin 1971: 91-93; Krech 1979: 106-109). This situation was intensified in 1840, with the opening of Peel's River Post (later called Fort MacPherson) near the head of the Delta.

Beginning in 1848, the search for the missing Third Franklin Expedition again brought the Royal Navy into the eastern Beaufort Sea. John Richardson returned, travelling east from the Mackenzie in search of his former captain. He again visited Nuvurak, which without comment he described as "a small village of <u>seven or eight huts</u>" (Richardson 1851: 254, emphasis mine), implying that it had halved in size since 1826. Within a few years he was followed by Pullen (Pullen 1979) and M'Clure, the latter expedition producing three published journals (Armstrong 1857; Miertsching 1967; M'Clure 1969). M'Clure, in particular, visited what was presumably a Nuvorugmiut village of about 100 people, at or near Warren Point (Armstrong 1857: 150; M'Clure 1969: 85-87), while all along the Tuktoyaktuk Peninsula "... everywhere I see Eskimo huts on shore..." (Miertsching 1967: 55). The M'Clure expedition also reported one reason, beyond fear of the Loucheux, why the Inuit remained aloof from the trade at Peel's River Post. On two occasions they were told that Indians trading there had been poisoned by drinking "fire water" (Armstrong 1857: 151, 164).

They did not stay aloof for long. In 1852 the first Mackenzie Inuit visited both Peel's River Post and its subsidiary, LaPierre House, and within three or four years a fairly lively trade had begun (see McGhee 1974: 2-3; Krech 1979: 109-110). Hostility with the Loucheux was a strong limiting factor throughout the 1850s (HBC, B/200/b/33: 45), but by 1860 there was a request for another assistant at the post "now that so many Esquimaux come to the Fort" (HBC, B/200/b/34: 10-11). This trade appears to have focused on the Mackenzie River Inuit proper (Kittegaryumiut and Kopugmiut), and there are indications that more easterly groups like the Nuvorugmiut and Avvaqmiut were being denied easy access to Peel's River Post by their bellicose western neighbours (see McGhee 1974: 3-4). Instead, most of their trade was still with Fort Good Hope, through Indian intermediaries. In 1855, Robert Campbell of Fort Good Hope reports sending off a party of Indians to open direct trade with the "Esquimaux of Liverpool Bay" (HBC, B/200/b/32: 102). Robert MacFarlane, also of Fort Good Hope, had high expectations of the advantages of direct trade, writing "...there is reason to believe that when (the fur trade's) benefits are felt by these people, and they become in a manner dependent on the Whites for their wants, from their well known industrious habits they would exert themselves in a far greater degree than the Indians and there is also reason to believe that this trade would at no distant date embrace the whole Eastern Esquimaux indirectly through their Countrymen of Liverpool Bay" (HBC, B/200/b/31: 66).

After two exploratory journeys in the late 1850s, in 1861 MacFarlane succeeded in establishing Fort Anderson on the Anderson River (Stager 1967). It was better known at the time as "Eskimo Fort", and was the first Hudson's Bay Company post established to trade specifically with Inuit anywhere in Canada. Among his visitors was the eccentric Oblate missionary Emile Petitot, who has left colourful but difficult accounts of his activities and observations (Petitot 1970, 1981). Apparently, both Nuvorugmiut and Avvaqmiut were directly involved with the Fort Anderson trade. Stefansson (1914:349) reports that both groups had the same name for MacFarlane ("Misipalla"), and even the same mistaken version of it ("Misimikpala"), suggesting that their intimacy with the trader and his post was mutual. Unfortunately, the Hudson's Bay Company reports never distinguish the Nuvorugmiut by name. Instead, they refer to the Anderson River, Liverpool Bay, or Cape Bathurst people on one hand (also called "Eastern Esquimaux"), and the Mackenzie River people on the other. Probably, Nuvorugmiut were included in both groups. However, they are more likely to have been confused with the Avvaqmiut of Anderson River/Cape Bathurst, whom they resembled in most respects (McGhee 1974: 18), including the most visually obvious; unlike their western neighbours, the men of both groups had facial tattoos and, apparently, rarely wore labrets (Franklin 1971: 120, 214;

Richardson 1851: 355; Armstrong 1857: 193-194; Petitot 1970: 176, Fig. 21).

In 1866 Fort Anderson was abandoned. It had never been well situated, and there were major problems keeping it supplied from Fort Good Hope. Moreover, revenues were declining (Stager 1967). Orders for its abandonment were carried out in secret because of fear of Inuit anger, Chief Factor Hardisty noting that "care should be taken that the Esquimaux receive no intimation of our designs before they leave for the Sea Coast" (HBC, B/200/b/35: 75).

The year before, the Inuit had been hit by their first major epidemic, variously described as scarlet fever or measles. According to Petitot (1970: 140): "... because of the measles, all the Eskimos, fleeing from the shores of Anderson River, sought refuge on the shores of Liverpool Bay and Franklin Bay.... There were 28 deaths from the measles on the Anderson River... and no one can say how many died around the shores of the Arctic Sea." The Hudson's Bay Company reported that "A rumour also has reached Good Hope, that the Esquimaux were exasperated against the Whites, on account of the number of their people who had died of the Measles, which they imagined was caused by the "bad medicine" of the Whites" (HBC, B/200/b/35: 94). Three years later, "typhus or some nervous fever" was reported (Petitot 1970:140), and the Mackenzie Inuit were never again without the immediate threat of infectious disease.

The end of the Fort Anderson trade seems to have caused real economic disruption to people now accustomed to the Hudson's Bay Company and what it had to offer. The Company had hoped that the "Anderson Esquimaux" would "trade their furs with the Good Hope Indians, as they did formerly" (HBC, B/200/b/35: 94). However, Petitot counted 250 "Anderson Eskimos" trading alongside Mackenzie River people at Peel's River Post in 1866 (Petitot 1970: 136). By the winter of 1869/70, the two groups, both suffering from disease, were reported wintering together, "camped on the ice hunting seals" (HBC, B/200/b/38:22).

Disastrous as previous events had been, the late 1880s can be seen, in hindsight, as the beginning of the end. As early as the 1860s, rumours of whaling ships had reached the Hudson's Bay Company at Peel's River (HBC, B/200/b/36: 165; B/200/b/37: 81), but it was not until 1888 that the first ship is known to have entered Canadian waters. It was part of the American

Beaufort Sea whaling fleet, based in Seattle (Bockstoce 1986). Since 1819, American whalers had been working their way north and east from Bering Strait. Because of the distances involved, they were forced to overwinter in order to make a successful voyage, and this appears to have greatly increased their destructive effect. In 1890, three ships wintered at Herschel Island, and by 1894 the number was up to 15. Smaller numbers wintered as far east as Cape Bathurst (Martell et al. 1984: 26-27; Bockstoce 1986). In the 25 years between 1890 and the First World War, the whalers took about 1500 bowhead whales from Canadian waters (Martell et al. 1984: 27), and incidentally destroyed the Mackenzie Inuit, both as a people and a culture.

The impact of the whalers could be felt in every aspect of life. The naturalist Frank Russell travelled through the area early in the whaling era, and is one of our best witnesses to some of the more benign effects. The whalers were able to import large quantities of inexpensive trade goods, completely outflanking the Hudson's Bay Company, with its interior supply routes (see Stefansson 1922: 104-106). In 1893 (?) Russell (1898: 141-142) met a group of Inuit west of the Mackenzie who had been trading with the whalers at Herschel. They had several large bags of flour ("as much as some northern posts receive for a year's allowance"), a new wall tent, and syrup and coffee ("articles quite unknown in the interior"). "Anderson River Eskimos" met on the north Yukon coast also had coffee, flour and syrup, while repeating rifles were almost universally employed (Russell 1898: 191). Of Inuit he met at Herschel, one of the men "...wore a new sombrero with a very broad brim. Others had miscellaneous odds and ends combined with their native costumes, with the effect on the beholder of having discarded a portion of their apparel and substituted an incongruous textile fabric to mark the loss. Several wore tight-fitting red flannel drawers over their deerskin trousers" (Russell 1898: 146).

Much more serious were the effects of prostitution and alcohol abuse. One of the whalers, it is reported, was nicknamed "the kindergarten captain" after his erotic fascination with young children (Bockstoce 1986: 277). Jenness (1964: 14) reports that the introduction of alcohol, and of "home" brewing, converted Herschel and the Mackenzie Delta into "a hive of debauchery" within a year.

Along with the whalers came large numbers of Alaskan and even

Siberian Eskimo, refugees from a disastrous decline in caribou stocks in their own homelands. Known as "Nunatama" (see Burch 1976), they were drawn by the riches of the Mackenzie Delta area, the prospect of employment by the whalers, and "the acquaintance which had subsisted from ancient times between the Nunatama and the Kogmolik (Mackenzie Inuit)" (Harrison 1908: 80). Stefansson (1914: 195) reported in the early days of the present century that because of the influx of Nunatama, "the Mackenzie population is becoming mixed in blood, is already deeply influenced in its culture, and has taken up many strange words in the spoken language."

Unfortunately, the Nunatama exported their own problem. The native Mackenzie Inuit were considered poor caribou hunters, so it was, by and large, Nunatama who were employed to hunt for the whaling ships. The need for hunters was so great that in 1894 and 1895 most of the inhabitants of Point Barrow, Alaska, were employed at Herschel, as were nearly one hundred people from Point Hope (Bockstoce 1986: 274). Approximately 50,000 caribou were killed (Martell et al. 1984: 43). Although Bockstoce (1986: 275) denies that this hunting had any major effect on caribou populations, it seems clear that it did. The Mackenzie Delta area had been well supplied with caribou before the whaling era, yet in 1906, Stefansson subsisted with his Inuit companions entirely on fish, noting that "The Eskimos say that before the whalers came and induced the Eskimos to kill so many caribou to feed the ships, there used to be considerable numbers just east of the Mackenzie" (Stefansson 1922: 182). The Mackenzie Inuk, Nuligak, born in the 1890s, did not see his first caribou until he was 16 (Nuligak 1966: 77-83).

But the worst gift of the whalers was disease. After various preliminary epidemics, two major measles outbreaks in 1900 and 1902 put the final seal on the fate of the Mackenzie Inuit (Jenness 1964: 14). Kittigazuit, Nuvurak, and other villages were finally abandoned at this time (Stefansson 1914: 24, 349). Police reports show that the Mackenzie Inuit population fell from an estimated 2500 people in 1850, to 250 people in 1905, further reduced to 150 in 1910 (Usher 1971: 175). One survivor, Nuligak, remembers,

> That summer the Kitigariuit (sic) people fell ill
> and many of them died. Almost the whole tribe

perished, for only a few families survived.
During that time, two of the Eskimos spent all
their time burying the dead.... Corpses were set
on the ground uncoffined, just as they were.
Since I could not count at the time I shall not
attempt to give a number; but I know that when
the people left for Kiklavak (Richardson's Island)
they were but a handful compared to the number
they had been. It was 1902....

Winter came, and one day we saw a huge
pack of wolves out at sea on the ice, heading
east. There were so many of them that the last
ones were still in front of us when the leaders
had disappeared on the eastern horizon. It was
said that they had feasted on the bodies left on
the Kitigariuit land...(Nuligak 1966: 27).

Changes in the Nuvorugmiut Economy

Something can be described of the subsistence economy of the
Nuvorugmiut from historic accounts for two periods in their history. In
1848, they were visited at Nuvurak by John Richardson of the Royal Navy,
who spoke to one of the men through an interpreter. He learned that the
people of Nuvurak did not "wander far from their winter station at Point
Atkinson," and "dread their turbulent countrymen" around the mouth of the
Mackenzie (Richardson 1851: 257-258). Their subsistence round was divided
into four seasons. In the summer, they "hunt rein-deer and water-fowl on
the neighbouring flats," and in autumn "chase the whale during one month or
six weeks." The people then live with their families in the village "during
the dark winter months." Finally, in spring they "travel sea-ward on the ice
to kill seals, at which time they dwell in snow-houses" (Richardson 1851:
257).

The observations of Richardson and other mid-nineteenth century
explorers, although limited to the summer sailing season, tend to confirm
this account. Thus Richardson arrived at Nuvurak on August 5, to find the
village nearly abandoned. He learned, however, that people would be

11

congregating very soon for whaling, and in fact on the next day reported "We now had a pretty numerous body around us" (Richardson 1851: 260). Later, he specifically identifies August as the month devoted to whaling (Richardson 1851: 346). In 1850, Robert M'Clure visited a Nuvorugmiut village at or near Warren Point, just west of Nuvurak. He found it, on August 24, to be occupied by about 100 people. The chief "had a quantity of blubber and whalebone to barter with the western people, for his people had killed three whales in the present season" (M'Clure 1969: 87; see also Armstrong 1857: 150-151).

The whales the Nuvorugmiut hunted were bowhead whales (<u>Balaena mysticetus</u>), the same prey as their Avvaqmiut neighbours, and the American whaling fleet. More westerly groups in the Delta depended instead on the much smaller beluga whale, although they did sometimes take bowhead as well. A mature bowhead can attain 20 m in length, and easily weighs 40,000 kg (Banfield 1974: 283; Rick 1980: 111). It is likely, however, that the Nuvorugmiut took mainly immature animals of less than 10 m length (see McCartney and Savelle 1985: 45). In the western Arctic, bowhead winter in the Bering Sea area and migrate each spring to summering grounds in the eastern Beaufort Sea. An analysis of whaling ship logs suggests that the eastward migration tends to take animals comparatively far from shore, arriving in the Amundsen Gulf area by July. They then move in a leisurely fashion south and west, passing by Cape Bathurst and along the Tuktoyaktuk Peninsula, frequenting inshore waters, especially those in the "20-25 fathom ground" (Fraker and Bockstoce 1980). It was at this time of year that the Inuit hunt was made, and under open water conditions. By contrast, Alaskan native whalers hunted actively migrating whales along ice leads, a much more productive technique (Burch 1981), but clearly impossible in the eastern Beaufort Sea.

As we have already seen, the Nuvorugmiut are poorly distinguished in the historical record, so that it is difficult to determine the success or importance of whaling in their economy from the few pertinent records. However, a comparison with the neighbouring Avvaqmiut is revealing. The subsistence economy of these people appears to have been quite similar to that of the Nuvorugmiut (McGhee 1974: 18; MacFarlane 1891; 1905), but it is better known in detail. From the size and location of their whaling villages near Cape Bathurst (see Richardson 1851: 268; Armstrong 1857: 172-175; Miertsching 1967: 59; Pullen 1979: 114-115, 120), it is likely that the Avvaqmiut were more successful whalers than the Nuvorugmiut, and one certainly obtains that impression from the historical sources. Thus Richardson (1851: 348) specifically cites Cape Bathurst, but not Nuvurak, as a major whaling location. Richardson (1851: 267) learned that in some summers the Avvaqmiut "kill two black whales, very rarely three, and sometimes they are altogether unsuccessful." MacFarlane (1905: 730) gives a slightly lower estimate: "The Eskimos who frequented Fort Anderson succeeded most seasons in killing one large whale, but seldom as many as two. Plenty reigned for many months as a result." Similar or lower figures, then, seem likely for the Nuvurogmiut, if they were not, in fact, included in MacFarlane's estimate. The year in which Nuvorugmiut at Warren Point succeeded in killing three whales (M'Clure 1969: 87) would appear to have been exceptional.

If Richardson and the Royal Navy are our prime sources on the Nuvorugmiut around the middle of the nineteenth century, Stefansson is far more informative about the end of the aboriginal period. Stefansson did not come North until 1906, a time when the culture of the Nuvorugmiut, and the Mackenzie Inuit generally, was already practically extinct. His account (Stefansson 1914), however, is retrospective, based on the memory of several informants, chiefly a woman named Guninana, born at Nuvurak about 1880. Most of his observations relate to the 1880s and 90s, although sometimes it is not clear exactly what period is being recalled. His account was never edited, and is highly disjointed, being for the most part random diary notes. Nonetheless, it is difficult to overestimate its importance.

The most obvious difference between the early and late accounts is a shift away from whaling. The Nuvorugmiut apparently gave up whaling in the mid-1880s, Stefansson (1914: 350) writing that "As late as twenty-five years ago, the people of Nuvurak used to go out in boats looking for bowhead whales, but they never got any since Guninana remembers, she is thirty or a little over." There is no indication as to why this occurred. It was not competition with the American whalers, who did not enter the area for several more years. When they did, they reported that whales were "as thick as bees" (Bockstoce 1986: 256).

Instead of bowhead, the Nuvorugmiut are described as depending on the basic triad of caribou, seals, and fish. Of course, they had always depended in part on these animals, but now, with the cessation of whaling, this dependence, particularly on caribou, may have become intensified. Thus, travelling east from the mouth of the Mackenzie, Stefansson (1914: 14) notes that the "first village of real sealers was that at Point Atkinson, called Nuvorak." The main sealing season, as before, seems to have been "the dark days of winter," when seals were taken in nets from the Nuvurak village site (Ibid.: 350). But it was caribou which, from Stefansson's account, appears to have filled the void left by whaling. The evidence is as follows. The East Channel Kittegaryumiut, we know, had a "scheduling problem," in that the best season for caribou hunting conflicted with the beluga season. As Stefansson (Ibid.: 356) writes, "Only those of the Kittegaryuit who neglected the white whale hunt, and they were few, got any considerable number of deer during the season of suitability for clothing; hence their need to buy skins." They bought them from the Nuvorugmiut (Ibid.: 355), who evidently had a surplus. Moreover, the season of hunting which furnished the bulk of the skins used for clothing was "between the first week of August and the middle of September" (Ibid.:149). It will be noted that this conflicts perfectly with the old bowhead whaling season.

Instead of whaling, then, the late nineteenth-century Nuvorugmiut appear to have devoted this crucial period of the year to intensive caribou hunting. Stefansson's descriptions of Nuvorugmiut life in fact concentrate very largely on caribou hunting. Interestingly, these descriptions include the earliest historical mention of the Kugaluk area.

> The Nuvorugmiut hunted caribou towards the foot
> of Liverpool Bay and also spent part of the
> autumn there annually in fishing (Ibid.: 14).
>
> It was rare any Nuvurak people joined the
> Kittegaryuit for the summer beluga hunt.... In
> summer, they devoted their main energies to the
> caribou hunt, chiefly to the east of Nuvurak....
> There were many caribou, especially on the
> islands between Nuvurak and the river that runs

out of the Eskimo lakes.... Some who intended to
winter on the Kugaluk to hunt foxes, etc., also
hunted caribou there. There were several caribou
spearing places, yet much hunting was with bows.
Meat was thrown away and only the skins taken,
when animals were killed far from camp. Large
quantities of dried meat were made; umiaks used
to return deep loaded with dry meat, fat, and
skins from the hunt in the fall (Ibid.: 355-356).

Problems and Research Goals

Before the Kugaluk site was tested and its approximate age known, it
was hoped in a general way that its excavation would throw light on a
rather poorly known people, their way of life and their relationship with
other groups. Now that excavation is complete and a reasonable artifact
collection has been made, it can be asserted that the site almost certainly
dates to sometime between 1850 and 1875, and probably about 1860 (see
Chapter Three). This allows us to focus our research goals, particularly in
light of the historic information presented above.

As we have seen, there are two quite different descriptions of the
Nuvorugmiut economy. These descriptions are separated by approximately 40
years, during which time the Nuvorugmiut underwent major, and tragic,
changes. One of these changes, certainly, was the abandonment of whaling,
for reasons which are unknown. A straight, possibly naive, reading of the
historical information seems to lead to the conclusion that caribou hunting
was simply substituted for whaling during the important August early
September period. This may have resulted in the territorial expansion of a
"community (which) does not wander far from their winter station on Point
Atkinson" (Richardson 1851: 257), to one we know was hunting at least as
far south as the Kugaluk River.

The historical data, however, are very imperfect. Certainly there are
biases, reflecting (at least) changes in the nature of contact in the middle
and late nineteenth century. Thus Richardson and M'Clure, exploring the
coast of the Tuktoyaktuk Peninsula in August, met and talked with whale
hunters in their coastal villages. They had no contact with the interior, or

even with the Eskimo Lakes, which were not even minimally explored until 1889 (deSainville 1984). Their conversations with natives were short, few in number, and limited by the skill of an interpreter. By contrast, Stefansson based his observations on much more extensive and intimate contacts, involving more people over a greater area of land, and over the entire seasonal round. He was himself fluent (or in the process of becoming fluent) in Inuktitut, and actually wintered on the Eskimo Lakes. It is possible, then, that the importance of whaling in mid-nineteenth century accounts is exaggerated by the location and season of contact. Stefansson's description of a much more interior-oriented, caribou-hunting people may have been almost as applicable to the early contact Nuvorugmiut as to their late nineteenth century descendants.

Dating to within a short time of Richardson's voyage, and with an interior location, the Kugaluk site is well suited for an investigation of this suggestion. Analysis concentrates largely on architectural features, and particularly on the faunal material, in the hope of establishing the subsistence economy at the site, and then of placing it within a larger, regional context. The analysis of artifactual material occupies a lesser place, and is primarily concerned with establishing the age of the site, and investigating the degree of change in the material tool kit. Overall, the site provides a snap-shot picture of a traditional Arctic hunting society on the eve of massive change.

CHAPTER TWO

THE EXCAVATION AND STRUCTURE OF THE KUGALUK SITE

Previous Archaeological Work in the Area

The only Nuvorugmiut site to have previously seen any significant work
is the main village of Nuvurak, at Point Atkinson. Unfortunately, almost all
of the excavating (or collecting) was done in a haphazard fashion by
untrained "pot hunters," and the site has since been entirely destroyed by
land subsidence and wave action (see McGhee 1974: 26). In the 1920s, Knud
Rasmussen of the Fifth Thule Expedition purchased nearly 700 specimens,
excavated by local people (Mathiassen 1930: 7-19). Stylistically, they
indicate the site to have been occupied for at least three hundred years
prior to Richardson's visit, and at the same time are quite similar to
specimens later excavated at Kittigazuit (McGhee 1974). Another collection
from Nuvurak is held by the Ethnology Section of the Royal Ontario
Museum, collected in 1934 from an erosion beach (Catalogue H.C. 3444-3500).
It numbers about a hundred specimens, and has not been described. Finally,
in 1970, Gordon excavated a few graves found still intact in the area behind
the beach (Gordon 1971). Other Nuvorugmiut sites have been recently
located on the Tuktoyaktuk Peninsula (LeBlanc 1987), but have not yet been
investigated. As at Pt. Atkinson, most are rapidly being destroyed by land
subsidence.

More work has been done around the East Channel. Four large village
have been investigated, most notably Kittigazuit itself (McGhee 1974).
Artifact analysis and radiocarbon assays indicate this very major site to have
been occupied from about A.D. 1500 until its abandonment in 1902. From a
stylistic point of view it can be considered the Mackenzie Inuit "type site,"
not only because of its size and importance, but because of the precedence
McGhee's publication takes in the literature of the area. Slightly earlier and
just up-stream are Radio Creek (McGhee 1974) and Cache Point (Stromberg
1987), while immediately across the river is Kopuk (or Gupuk), chief village
of the Kopugmiut (Arnold 1987). Final reports are not yet available for
Cache Point and Kopuk, but the inhabitants of all four appear to have had a
marked dependence on beluga whales, while artifact similarity is strong.
Other sites which can probably be associated with East Channel people are

17

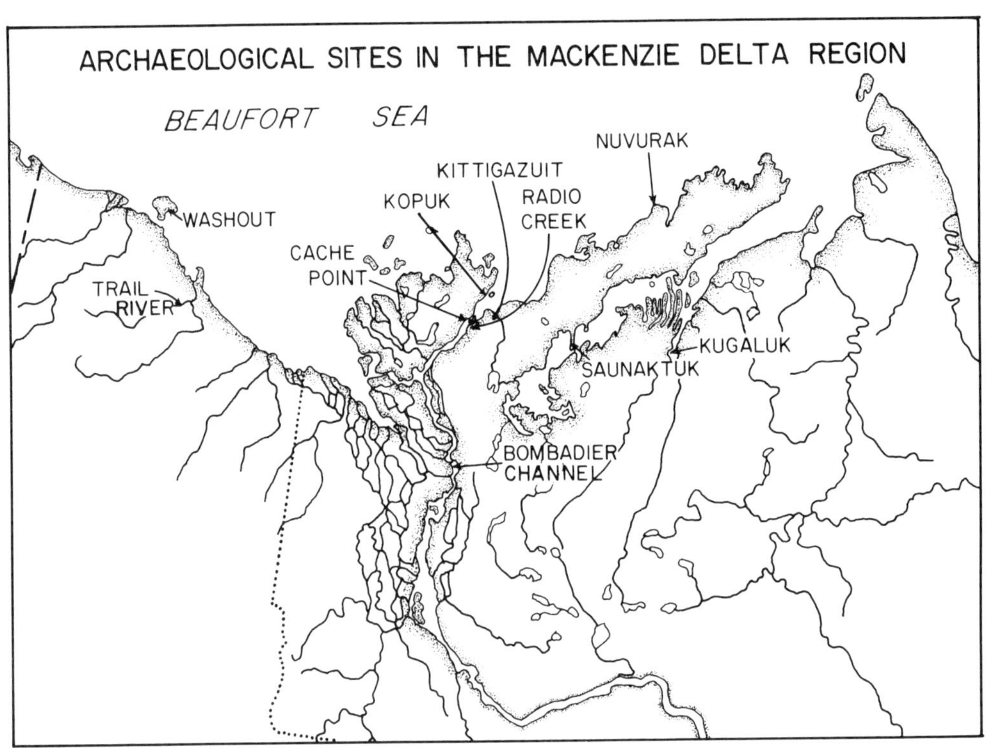

the Bombadier Channel site (Arnold 1986a), and Saunaktuk (Arnold 1986b). The former is a salvaged grave site, probably dating to the 1870s, located near Inuvik. Saunaktuk is closer to the Kugaluk area, in the "upper" or western Eskimo Lakes. It comprises several winter houses dating to around A.D. 1500.

Further west again, archaeologists have located a number of Inuit sites in the northern Yukon, including at least one (Trail River) which has seen some excavation (LeBlanc 1987).

It is difficult to synthesize data from these sites into any detailed prehistory of the Mackenzie Inuit. With the notable exceptions of Kittigazuit and Radio Creek (McGhee 1974), no major site excavation has yet been reported in more than a preliminary fashion. However, the Mackenzie Inuit presumably share the Thule culture origin common to all Inuktitut/Inupiat speakers, which implies a north or west Alaskan origin about 1000 years ago. Sites like Washout on Herschel Island (Yorga 1979) probably represent an early stage of Inuit colonization in the area, still with a generalized western Thule cultural affiliation. McGhee's (1974) work at Kittigazuit and Radio Creek demonstrates that the reasonably distinctive constellation of traits which identify the Mackenzie Inuit had been developed by the mid-fifteenth century. On an economic level, in the East Channel this means an adaptation to a distinctive and localized river estuary environment, with its attendant focus on beluga hunting and fishing. This is less true at Nuvurak, where something much closer to the basic Thule economy was retained, although there must have been a shift from ice-lead to open water whaling. On a stylistic level, we can infer the comparatively rapid development of distinctive artifact styles and types embracing the whole area, at least in so far as it is presently known. McGhee (1974: 86-93) has stressed, in particular, the importance of relations with west Alaska. Contact must have persisted over most of the prehistoric period, in part through the kind of trading networks known historically (Petitot 1970: 214-216).

Environmental Setting

The Kugaluk area is ecotonal in location, lying at the cross-roads between the Arctic and Subarctic, and between the interior and the coast. On most maps the tree-line is plotted a few kilometers north of the site, although the immediate area is willow tundra with only the occasional stunted spruce tree (<u>Picea</u>) or even rarer tamarack (<u>Larix laricina</u>) in protected locations. Dense willow (<u>Salix</u>) thickets can be utterly impassable, and two metres or more high. Full open boreal forest conditions are to be found within a few dozen kilometers, along the lower Kugaluk River, and even the treeless north end of the estuary is well supplied with driftwood. The topography is well-drained and slightly rolling, under a heavy mantle of Pleistocene sediments (see Mackay 1963: 18-21, 145).

Although located on salt water, Kugaluk is essentially an inland site for purposes other than transportation, lying dozens of kilometers south of the open ocean. Terrestrial resources predominate, of which by far the most important are barrenground caribou (_Rangifer tarandus groenlandicus_). The earliest historical references to the Kugaluk area, in fact, have to do with caribou hunting (Nuligak 1966: 72, 77-83; Stefansson 1914: 355-356). Animals found in the area are part of the Bluenose herd. They winter south of the study area, calving in mid to late May on the tundra 150 km to the east, around the base of the Cape Bathurst peninsula (Martell et al. 1984: 41-42). Badly decimated by hunters for the American whaling fleet around the turn of the century, the Bluenose herd is only now recovering in this western part of its range. According to a life-long inhabitant of the Kugaluk area, there were no caribou at all when he was a child there in the 1930s, and the first animals did not reappear until the early 1960s. Occasional caribou are now to be found nearly year-round, although they are only abundant during the spring and August migrations. The Bluenose herd presently numbers about 35,000 animals (Martell et al. 1984: 42), but would have been much larger in the last century. Other species in the Kugaluk area include barrenground grizzly (_Ursus arctos_), and the occasional black bear (_U. americanus_) and moose (_Alces alces_). Nesting waterfowl are abundant in the estuary during the summer.

The waters of Kugaluk estuary are brackish, and at low tide are potable due to discharge from the Miner and Kugaluk rivers. They support a range of anadromous, fresh, and salt water fish, of which whitefish (_Coregonus_ sp.) are the most abundant. During the open-water season the occasional beluga (_Delphinapterus leucas_) wanders into the estuary, and there are also a few ringed seals (_Phoca hispida_).

Site Excavation and Structure

The Kugaluk site was found during helicopter reconnaissance in 1984, and excavated over the course of the next two summers. Extensive shovel-testing prior to excavation showed that it consisted, at minimum, of a very thin sub-surface scatter of animal bone and associated dark humic soil, extending as much as 80 m from the grassy bank into which the three houses were dug. There were several discrete, localized concentrations of artifactual and faunal material, and it was on these, as well as the houses, that excavation focused. One house and all of these apparent outside

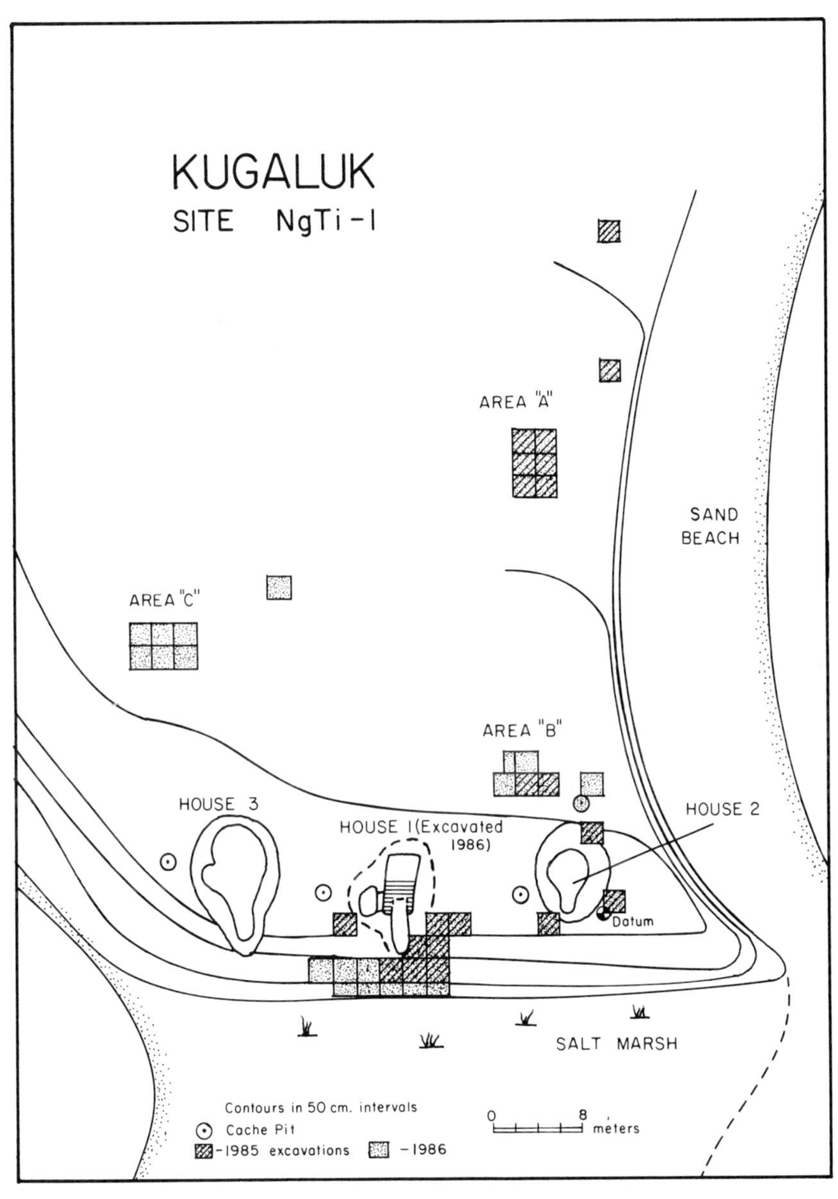

KUGALUK
SITE NgTi-1
AREA "A"
SAND
BEACH
AREA "C"
AREA "B"
HOUSE 3
HOUSE 1(Excavated
1986)
HOUSE 2
Datum
SALT MARSH
Contours in 50 cm. intervals
Cache Pit
-1985 excavations   -1986
0   8
meters

activity areas were excavated, totalling about 170 square-metres (Fig. 5).
Although this represents only a small fraction of the total site area, it is
estimated that a large percentage of the cultural material present at the site
was recovered.

Excavation proceeded using established techniques. Outside of the
house, 2-metre squares were the basic unit of excavation, with a single grid
established for the whole site. The location and depth of artifacts was
recorded within these squares, and excavation proceeded by trowel. All
faunal material was collected, again by square unit. Within the house,
instead of squares, the various rooms were used as excavation units; the
entrance passage, "front room," and rear sleeping platform. House floor
material was screened and floated. Finally, all site features were mapped
and photographed as they were revealed.

For descriptive purposes, the excavated portion of the site can be
divided into six areas; House 1, the midden associated with it, a cache pit,
and three outside activity areas, labelled "A," "B" and "C".

House 1: House 1 was the middle house in the row. Like the others, it had
a southward-facing entrance passage and was of single-family size, with a
floor space (including the sleeping platform but not the entrance passage) of
about 13.5 square-metres. It was chosen for excavation because it was the
best preserved, with the rear part of the east wall still partially standing.
This wall consisted of closely-spaced vertical posts about 10 cm in diameter,
with a pair of horizontal "stringers" running along the bottom, on the inside.
According to Stefansson (1922: 125), the walls would have sloped in toward
the top, to stabilize a stacked sod outer wall. The slumped remains of this
sod lay around the circumference of the house like a doughnut.

The first excavation level is shown in Figure 8,A. The roof sod has
been removed, revealing the collapsed roof and wall poles; evidently the
walls collapsed like those of a house of cards. Most of the logs were
rotten, and could be trowelled through. Some were better preserved,
however, and it was possible to determine that they had been cut using a
metal axe. A poorly-defined annex or store-room to one side showed no
sign of roofing, while the entrance passage showed an upper roofing level of
poles placed across the top of the walls. No attempt was made to excavate

FIGURE 6: **Kugaluk site ridge, at high tide**

FIGURE 7: **Screening house floor contents**

FIGURE 8

House 1, Kugaluk Site: First Two Excavation Levels

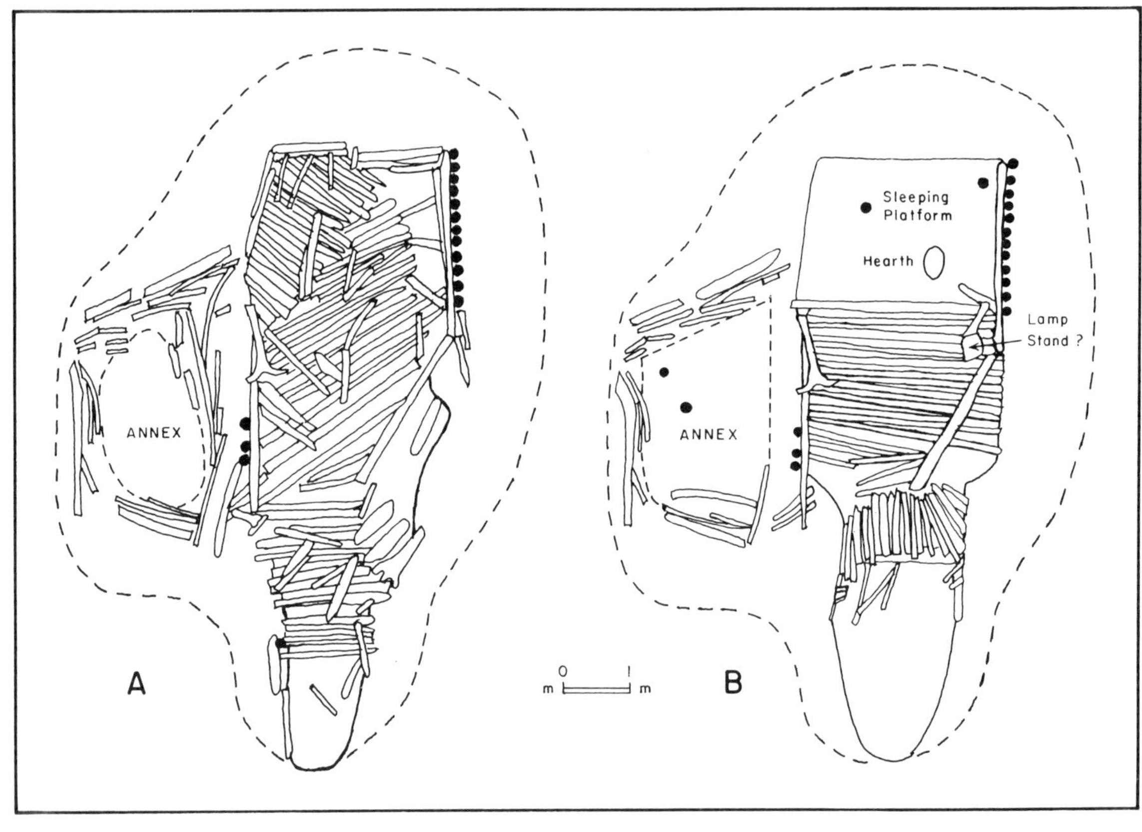

ANNEX
A

Sleeping
Platform
Hearth
Lamp
Stand ?
ANNEX
B
m 0   1 m

into the slumped sod ring about the house.

The second excavation level (Fig. 8,B) encompasses the uppermost house floor, except in the entrance passage. Here two roofing levels could be distinguished; the upper level already described, and a lower one consisting of short poles running along the length of the passage. The outer ends of these poles rested on a stout cross-piece embedded in the walls, while the inner brace was missing.

Floor 1 consisted of tightly-spaced poles 6-8 cm in diameter, running across the width of the floor. They were still in the round, unlike the plank floors of larger, probably more permanent houses described by Richardson (in Franklin 1971: 216) and Stefansson (1922: 88). To the rear was a sleeping platform raised about 30 cm above the level of the floor (Fig. 12). It was composed of packed earth with vestiges of a heather matting, and was approximately at ground level. The fact that it was of simple packed earth without a covering of poles or planks is another indication of the temporary nature of the house (see Petitot 1970: Fig. 29). A small hearth in the middle of the platform incorporated burned wall timbers, and is post-occupational. Toward the back of the floor was a flat pedestalled rock, which may have functioned as a lamp stand, although there was little evidence of burning or grease staining. Generally, debris was slight on Floor 1, and it was apparently occupied for only a short period of time.

The annex or store room proved to have stacked-sod walls, reinforced with wood, but with no vertical members. The stumps of two posts were visible on the earth floor. It, too, contained little debris, and did not communicate directly with the rest of the house.

The third excavation level (Fig. 9) includes the floor of the entrance passage and a second, lower house floor. The passage had an unpaved, sand floor which was fairly flat, reaching its maximum depth of about 80 cm below floor level just where it enters the house (see Fig. 12). The walls were in part of stacked sod reinforced with horizontal wood elements, and in part were simply dug into the bank.

Floor 2 was located directly beneath Floor 1, and was of packed earth, with a large, deep hearth in the middle. Large quantities of fish bone were associated with this floor, along with many small artifacts such as glass beads and metal fragments (see Tables 1-5 in the following two chapters).

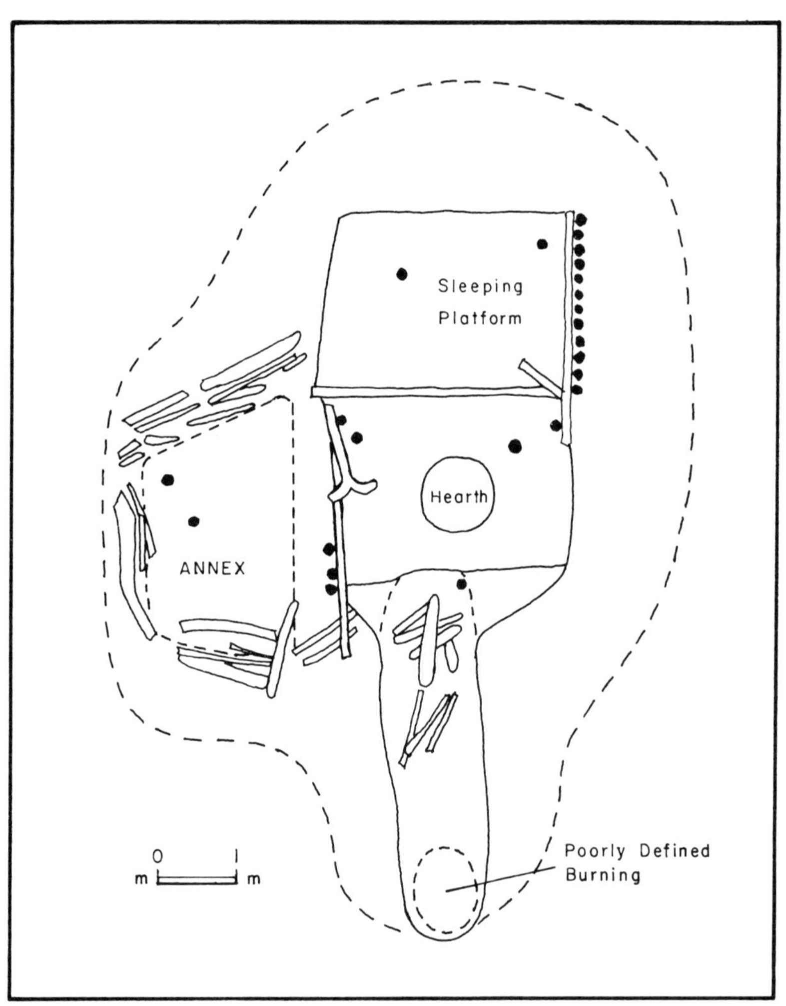

House 1, Kugaluk Site: Third Excavation Level

To some extent the high frequencies of such items are due to the fact that
Floor 2 was excavated using a screen, which aided greatly in the recovery of
small objects. Nonetheless, the contrast with Floor 1, which was also
excavated with a screen, is real, and suggests a much more intensive
occupation of the lower floor.

A second house (House 2) was also briefly tested. A 2-metre square in
one wall mound produced quantities of burned wood and charred earth. It
may be that this house burned down, presumably after it was abandoned.

Caches: Associated with each house was at least one small cache pit, visible
on the ground surface as a slight depression about a metre across. One was
excavated. It proved to be about 50 cm deep, and lacked any recognizable
wooden structure. Within was a quantity of bone, a few wooden fragments,
bone tool-making debitage, and a bark net float (see Fig. 15). The bones
were mostly caribou mandibles and crania, and likely represents garbage
kicked into the pit after it had been emptied of its original contents. It
was much less fragmentary than bone from any other area of the site.

Caches like these could have held only a small quantity of food, and
would have been accessible only during the summer.

Midden: A large garbage midden was located in front of House 1, extending
from the end of the entrance passage to the tide line, and probably beyond.
It had an average depth of 15-20 cm, and a maximum depth of 40 cm,
becoming thicker downslope. Most of the cultural material found at the site
was recovered from the midden, particularly in the case of the animal
remains. The matrix was of characteristically dark, organic soil, with a
great many pieces of wood. Downslope sections were water saturated, and
there was no evidence of internal stratification.

Extensive testing for further midden deposits associated with the other
two houses proved negative. It can only be supposed that these houses
were occupied for only a very brief period of time, if at all.

Area "A": North of the house row and near the edge of the east bank of the
island was the collapsed remains of what had probably been a stage or meat
rack. It consisted of logs, 10-15 cm in diameter and several metres

FIGURES 10 AND 11: **Two Views of House 1 after excavation**

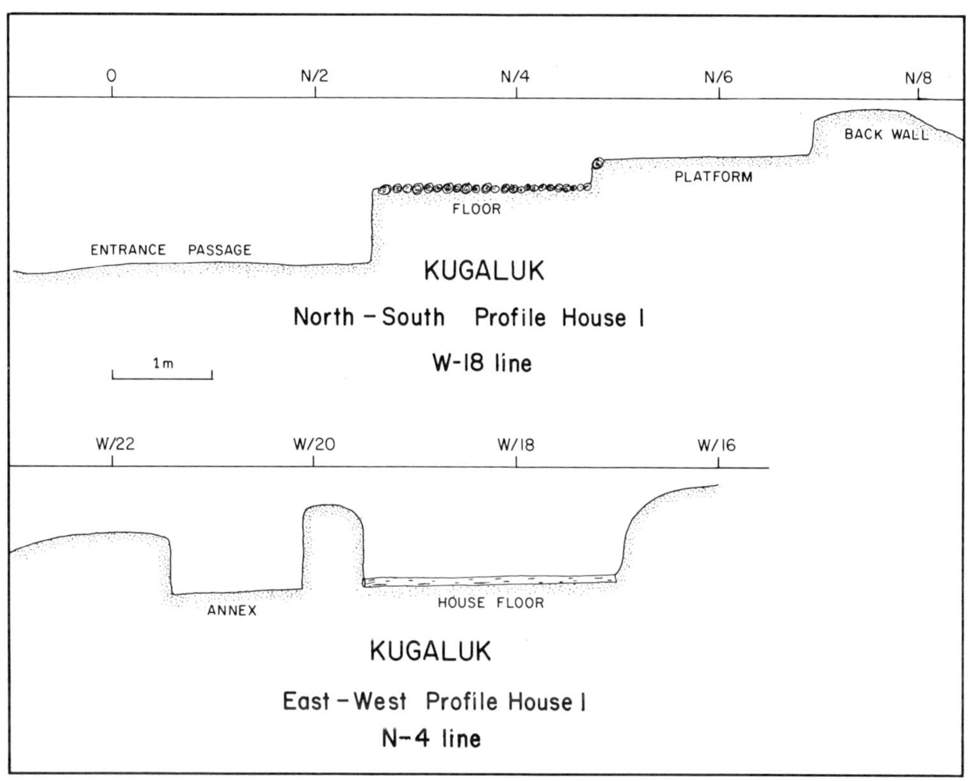

long, lying in a jumble over a considerable area. They were just below the surface, in some cases with grass growing directly from the wood, and their positions could sometimes be traced from the contours of the ground. About half of the area was excavated (24 square-metres) to sterile earth, at about 10-15 cm (Fig. 16). Cultural material was comparatively sparse, although a haphazard array of shallow post moulds was revealed. In some cases the wooden posts were still in place, wedged upright by pieces of bone. Also revealed was a large double-centred hearth. Beside it were an anvilstone, two hammerstones, and quantities of broken marrow bone.

FIGURE 13: Midden, with **in situ** Kayak Paddle

Area "B": Activity area "B" was more enigmatic. On the ground surface it consisted of a dense jumble of logs, some of them entirely unburied and bleached white by the sun (Fig. 17, upper). Beneath was a large, deep hearth, encircled by a great concentration of wood and antler chips, forming a dense carpet up to 7 cm deep (Fig. 17, lower). Cut bone and antler were also abundant, indicating considerable manufacturing activity. However, the comparative scarcity of recognizable tools or fragments (see Tables 1-4, Chapter 3) suggests that this bone, wood and antler working was mainly of a rough or preliminary sort. There was also evidence of metal-working, in the form of a large flattened piece of sheet metal, a lance point cut from such material, and many small iron fragments, two of which were found in the hearth itself. Around the perimeter of the hearth were the vertical stumps of four small wooden posts, from which a cauldron or pot might have been suspended (see Petitot 1970: 170). Three much larger posts seem to define the northern edge of the wood-and-antler chip concentration, while to the west an ill-defined sod hummock served the same function.

The circular formation of Area B, and the sod "wall" on the windward

FIGURE 14: **Excavations in Area A**

FIGURE 15: **The Excavated Cache**

side, could both be suggestive of some sort of tent structure. Against this
is Petitot's (1970: 170) observation that fires were built outside, rather than
within tents. The surface logs and masses of antler and wood chips also
argue against a tent interpretation. Instead, the low sod hummock and large
posts might represent a wind-break, sheltering an outside manufacturing
area, possibly in conjunction with a second stage or meat rack. The
wooden chips may represent not only manufacturing detritus, but also the
"excelsior" used in place of hand towels by the Mackenzie Inuit (see
Stefansson 1922: 148-149).

Area "C": Area C was located toward the northwestern extremity of the
site, in a flat area of, at present, dense willow growth. It was not
associated with any kind of once-standing structure, but seems to represent
a simple outside hearth. This hearth was again large and deep, and was
encircled by a thick, black deposit of charred bone (Fig. 18). Tools found
in this deposit were fragmentary, and were sometimes also charred. In an
area as well supplied with wood as Kugaluk, it is possible that the relatively
large-scale burning of bone was a means of garbage disposal. Despite this
evidence of burning, recognizable antler and bone tools were quite abundant,
particularly items used by men; hunting and fishing equipment, transportation
gear and men's tools (see Table 1-2, Chapter 3). It is likely that Area C
was the primary location for the manufacture and repair of such items. In contrast
with Area B, there was little evidence of metal working, or of the rough
adzing of antler and wood.

The Interpretation of Kugaluk Site Features

The structure of the Kugaluk site and its associated features suggest
that it was occupied over a period of several seasons. Probably the clearest
indications of cold-weather habitation are the "winter" houses, with their
recessed floors, sod and log walls, and cold-trap entrances. Such houses
represent a considerable outlay of labour, and would have been more or less
uninhabitable in the summer. According to ethnographic information, the
mid-19th century Avvaqmiut living immediately to the east of Kugaluk
retired to their "driftwood constructed huts, or winter houses" in early
December (MacFarlane 1905: 681). It seems likely that at least Floor 1 in

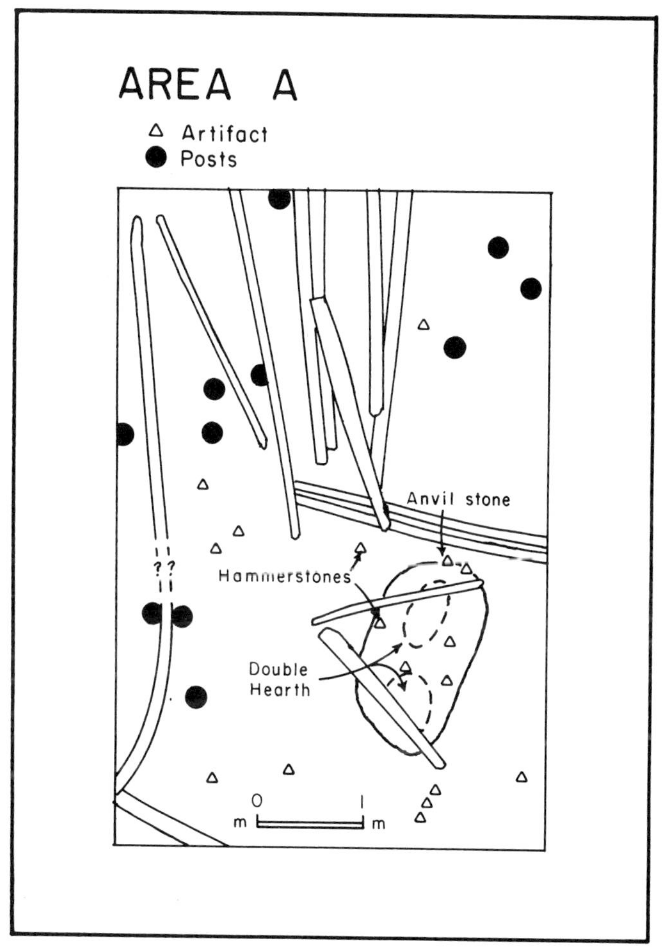

AREA A
Artifact
Posts
Anvil stone
Hammerstones
Double
Hearth
? ?
0
m
1
m

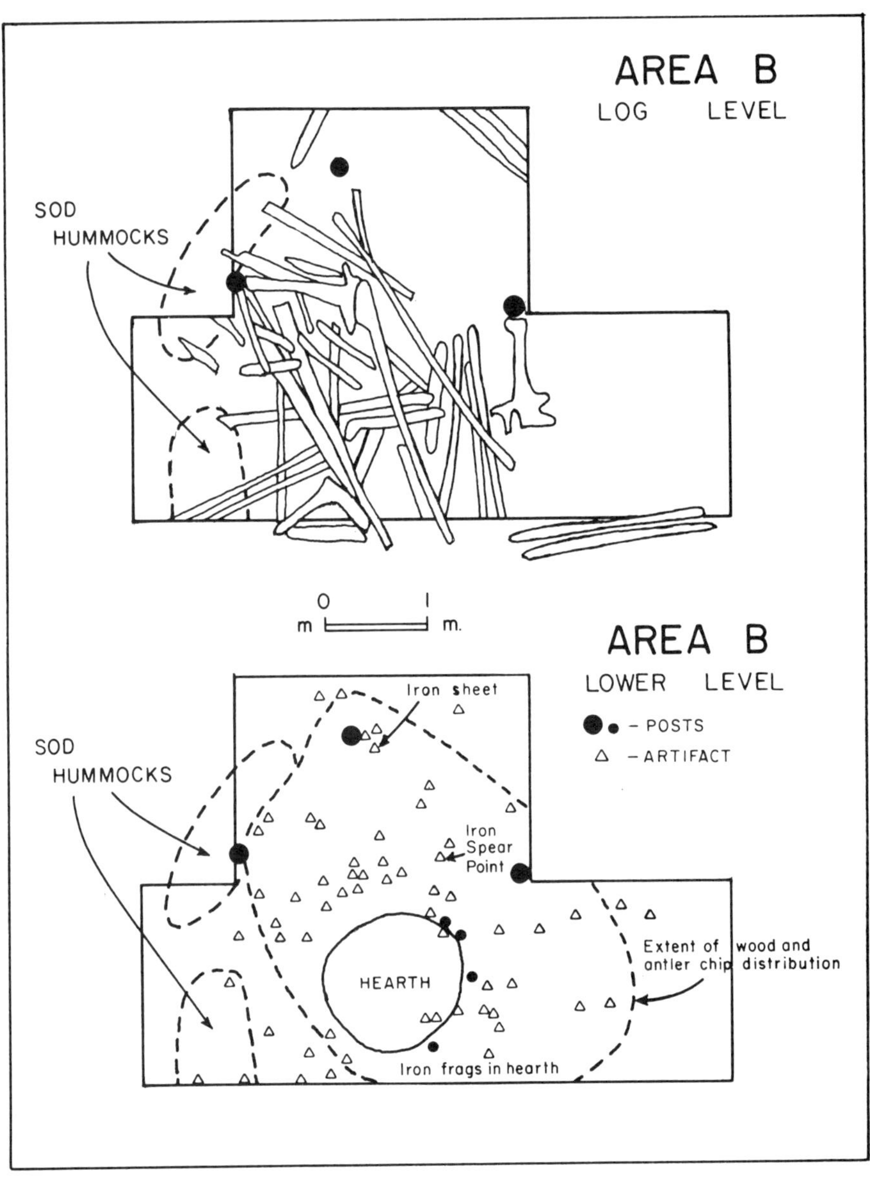

AREA B
LOG LEVEL
SOD HUMMOCKS
AREA B
LOWER LEVEL
● ● – POSTS
△ – ARTIFACT
SOD HUMMOCKS
Iron sheet
Iron Spear Point
Extent of wood and antler chip distribution
HEARTH
Iron frags in hearth
0
m
1
m.

the excavated house dates to a similar season. On the other hand, the
excavated house seems much smaller and more lightly built than coastal
cruciform houses described in ethnographic sources. There is thus the
possibility that it was meant to be occupied over only a comparatively brief
period, a suggestion we will take up again with reference to the faunal
material.

Indications of a warm-weather occupation are more abundant. They
include the small cache pits (which would have been accessible only when
the ground was unfrozen), and particularly the two large exterior hearths.
With their associated faunal and manufacturing debris, these hearths seem to
have been a focus of warm-weather, outdoor activity.

The lower excavated house floor, with its associated hearth, may also
relate to the warmer months of the year. Mackenzie Inuit winter houses
were normally heated with lamps, rather than open fires (Richardson 1851:
245, 348; Petitot 1970: 165). The difficulty with an open fire is ventilation,
which must be accomplished through an open smoke-hole or skylight, which
in turn draws off much of the heat in the house. Stefansson (1914: 136),
for instance, describes the Mackenzie Inuit _karigi_ or ceremonial house, as
heated with an open fire, noting that consequently it was too cold to be
much used in the winter. The presence of a hearth suggests that Floor 2
might also date to a summer or fall occupation, when this would not be a
serious problem. In a similar fashion, Richardson (1851: 255) describes an
"old crone sitting warming herself over a few embers" in a so-called winter
house at Nuvurak in August. The large size of the hearth relative to the
floor might even suggest its summer-time use as a smoke-house. However,
Floor 2 produced a great deal of cultural debris, mainly fish bone, but also
small artifacts such as glass beads and metal fragments. Certainly, it seems
to have been used much more intensively than the upper Floor 1.

It is difficult to determine whether the site was occupied once, or
returned to several times. The homogeneity of artifact styles (see Chapter
3), and the presence of similar trade goods in all site areas and both house
floors indicate that the site encapsules only a very brief period in the
history of the Nuvorugmiut. The lack of any vertical stratigraphy in the
midden points to a similar conclusion. Any further observations regarding
multiple occupations depend on the interpretation of the two house floors.

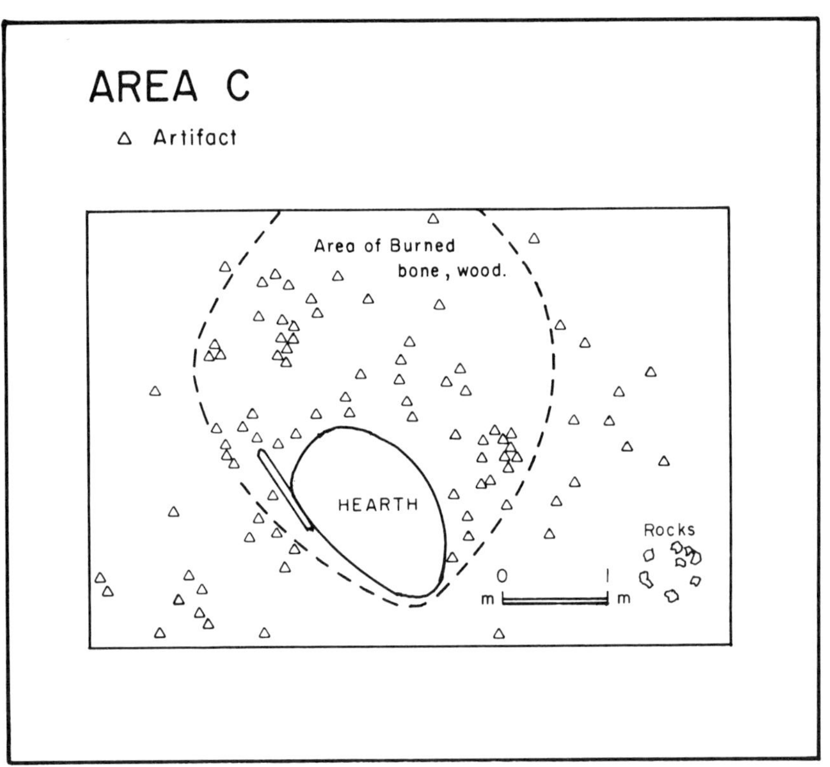

If they both represent winter occupations, then obviously the site was returned to at least once, and a new floor laid over the old one (see Stefansson 1922: 88). However, if the lower floor was lived on or used in some fashion during the summer and fall, then the entire occupation of the Kugaluk site might have occurred within the period of a single year. Analysis of the fish bone on the two floors tentatively supports the latter suggestion, as we shall see in Chapter 4.

CHAPTER THREE:

ARTIFACT DESCRIPTION AND ANALYSIS

The Kugaluk site excavations produced almost 1000 artifacts, of which the largest single category is debitage resulting from the manufacture of bone and antler tool blanks. This debitage represents several well-developed, systematic reduction strategies, but has already been described (Morrison in press), and so is not treated here. Artifact locations within the site are presented in Tables 1-4.

Sea Mammal Hunting Gear

Harpoon Heads

Two complete harpoon heads are both made of antler. One is a good example of the Nuwuk closed socket type (Ford 1959: 93), with the rivetted, triangular bone endblade still in place (Pl. 1,a). The line hole is drilled, the cross-section thick and ovate, and the spur symmetrically placed. The total length (including the endblade) is 70.5 mm; without the endblade it is 44.5 mm long.

The second specimen does not represent any well-defined type (Pl. 1,b). It is self-bladed, with a closed socket and an elongated, conical outline. The line hole has been drilled and is medially placed, while the cross-section is nearly round, and the spur is symmetrical. It is 66.5 mm long.

There are also seven harpoon head fragments, each consisting of a distal endblade prong. Five have a drilled rivet hole, and all could represent the Nuvuk type. They are made of antler.

Nuwuk closed socket harpoon heads date back to the Thule period (Ford 1959: Fig. 34; Morrison 1983a: 92-93), but are particularly characteristic of late prehistoric and historic Inuit cultures from Alaska to Coronation Gulf (Murdoch 1892: 221; Mathiassen 1930: 8; McGhee 1974: 45; Jenness 1946: 116; Morrison 1981: 262). The untyped specimen shows some similarities to nineteenth-century Kunana closed socket harpoon heads from western Victoria Island (McGhee 1972:76), and to Giddings's Type 1 harpoon heads from Nukleet in western Alaska (Giddings 1964: 38). Both

TABLE 1

LOCATION OF HUNTING AND FISHING GEAR: KUGALUK SITE

Item	Midden	House Fill	F-1	F-2	"A"	"B"	"C"	Cache	Misc.
Nuwuk harpoon head	1								
aberrant harpoon head	1								
harpoon head fragments	2	1					4		
harpoon endblade, stone		2					1		
, iron					1				
foreshaft							1		
socketpiece (?)							1		
lance heads, antler	2						1		
wound pin							1		
arrowheads, bone	1	1		1			1		
, antler	4	2			1	1	2		
, blanks	1	1							
bird bunts, bone	2						2		
, antler		1							
endblades, chert	1	1							
cutting board	1								
lance head, bone							1		
, stone	1						2		
, iron						1			
musket frizzen						1			
musket sear						1			
fish hook shank	1								
fish hook, iron				1					
, bone/antler	4	3		1					
, blank	1								
net gauges	1						1		
net sinkers, stone	4		1	1	1	2	10		
net floats, bark							1	1	
spear sideprong					1				

complete specimens, and for that matter the fragments, are of a size
suggestive of use in hunting small seals.

Harpoon Endblades

Three harpoon endblades are made of ground stone. Two are finished
and complete, and are slightly fluted in cross-section, with strongly bevelled
edges (Pl. 1,c-d). They have flat bases and hectagonal outlines, with two
points-of-juncture on each lateral margin. The third stone endblade is
evidently unfinished, with the lateral margins still showing evidence of
preliminary chipping. The two finished specimens are 36.5 and 40 mm long,
respectively, 18-19.5 mm wide, and about 3 mm thick.

A fourth endblade is made of iron (Pl. 1,e). It is triangular, with a
slightly concave base, and a thin, uniform cross-section, suggesting that it
was cut from sheet metal. The edges have not been sharpened, and it is
pierced by an iron rivet. Length: 49 mm; width: 26 mm; thickness: 1 mm.

Harpoon Foreshaft

A single complete foreshaft is made of antler (Pl. 1,f). It is of the
loose or moveable type, 245 mm long, with straight sides and a drilled,
laterally-placed line hole. The butt is conical, and the distal end perfectly
fits the socket of the Nuwuk harpoon head described above. Adjacent to
the line hole is a deeply incised spurred line which appears to be an
ownership mark.

Thule-style loose foreshafts like this one were designed to be used with
a throwing harpoon (Morrison 1983b: 69). In the Delta region, similar
examples made of wood and whale bone occur at Cache Point (Stromberg,
personal communication) and Pt. Atkinson (Mathiassen 1930: 8). Tentatively
identified specimens from Kittigazuit are quite different (McGhee 1974: 46).

Socket Piece

A single tentatively identified fragment seems to be from an antler
socket piece. The actual socket part appears to have been rather short,
protruding only 21 mm above the scarfed tang element. Specimens from
nearby sites such as Kittigazuit (McGhee 1974: 46), Radio Creek (McGhee
1974: 78), and Pt. Atkinson (Mathiassen 1930: Pl. 2,2) are similar but

considerably longer.

Lance Heads

At least two fixed antler lance heads were found at Kugaluk. One (Pl. 1,g) is nearly complete, 171 mm long, ovate but comparatively flat in cross-section, and has the blade slit cut through its greatest width. The tip is rounded, and the proximal end has been cut aslant for attachment to the shaft. There are two rivet holes to secure the blade, and one for the shaft. A second specimen is more fragmentary but seems nearly identical, while a broad, double-holed distal blade prong may be from a third specimen.

Fixed antler lance heads are a specifically eastern Arctic form, (Mathiassen 1927b: 36-37), and their presence at Kugaluk is surprising. Functionally similar weapons from Alaska and elsewhere in the Mackenzie Delta region consist either of a long wooden spear with a lashed chipped stone point (Murdoch 1892: 240; McGhee 1974: 48), or have a detachable wooden "foreshaft" to which a chipped stone point was affixed (Ford 1959: 105; Stanford 1976: 27). Lance heads were used in the hunting of large sea mammals, in this case probably beluga.

Wound Pin

What appears to be a fragment from an antler wound pin was recovered. It would have had a recessed bed beneath the expanded head. Similar specimens occur widely in recent Arctic cultures, and were used primarily in seal hunting (Ford 1959: 106; Jenness 1946: 120; Mathiassen 1927b: 40-41). They seem rare in the Mackenzie Delta area.

Terrestrial Hunting Gear

Bone and Antler Arrowheads

Twenty bone and antler arrowheads were found, including two antler blanks and four blunt bird arrowheads (described separately below). Four are made of bone (Pl. 1,h-j), and share a number of traits, particularly in the method of manufacture. They were made on a splinter or blank taken from one of the posterior ridges of a caribou metatarsal, as is witnessed by both the form of the finished arrowhead and from the manufacturing detritus (see Morrison in press). They have a trianguloid cross-section, with one margin representing the outer edge of the posterior ridge, and the other two margins being cut. One face shows a concavity representing the inner surface of the medullary cavity. Three are barbed, with two to three rather square barbs cut into one of the cut margins (rather than into the "back"). Tangs are conical and very sharp, with a smooth, sloping shoulder, and none shows any provision for the attachment of an endblade. Two complete specimens are 95 and 133 mm long, respectively.

Ten other specimens are made of antler, and again are all self-bladed (Pl. 1,k-m). Four have conical, nearly shoulderless tangs like those seen on the bone heads, while five have well-marked shoulders. Two of the latter also exhibit a pair of small symmetrical spurs on the tang. At least five were barbed (several are fragmentary), and again the barbs are consistently unilateral, numbering from one to five per specimen. Three specimens have lines incised along the edge of the barbing, and at least three of the more fragmentary specimens show evidence of re-working. Cross-sections range from nearly round to sharply biconvex, and complete lengths from 129.5 to 203 mm.

The antler arrowheads are typical of Thule to recent Inuit specimens from the western Arctic generally. The bone specimens are more distinctive, and may represent a "type" particular to the Mackenzie Delta area. Similar examples occur at Kittigazuit (McGhee 1974: 48), Pt. Atkinson (Mathiassen 1930: 9-10), and the Bombardier Channel site (Arnold 1986: 8). Moreover, Murdoch (1892: Fig. 188) illustrates an ethnographic specimen from Pt. Barrow which was described by his informants as coming from the "Kunmud'lin" or Mackenzie Inuit. McGhee (1974: 48) notes that they resemble Kutchin arrowheads from the lower Mackenzie-northern Yukon area, which were similarly made on metatarsal blanks (see LeBlanc 1984: 319). Many ethnographic arrowheads collected by MacFarlane from the Anderson River area are also made on metatarsal blanks, but differ in having large, barbed iron endblades (collections of the Smithsonian Institution, Anthropology Department).

Blunt Arrowheads

Of four blunt arrowheads, three were made on metatarsal blanks like those used for making pointed arrowheads. Each has a tri-lobate tip, and a round to triangular cross-section. Two have conical tangs set beneath sloping shoulders (Pl. 2,a-b), while the third has a drilled socket (Pl. 2,c). Because of the raw material, they are comparatively slender, with diameters of less than 10 mm. The longest specimen is 81.5 mm long. Technologically, they are very similar to the pointed bone arrowheads described above.

The one antler example is much larger and more typical of Inuit bird bunts (Pl. 2,d), with a maximum diameter of 21.5 mm. It has a four-lobed tip and a split-based tang, formed by cutting between drilled holes. One of the few decorated specimens in the collection, it is encircled by three pairs of incised lines.

Chipped Stone Arrowheads

Two chert point fragments are too small to be typed, and can only be tentatively identified.

Feather Cutting Board

A narrow slab of wood 142 mm long and 26 mm wide has a number of fine, straight cut marks on one surface (Pl. 2,g). One end is rounded and the other has been cut to an asymmetric, oblique point. The sides of the lateral margins are decorated with incised V-figures. Tapered-end boards like this are found at Kittigazuit (McGhee 1974: 53) and in western Alaskan sites (Giddings 1952: 81; 1964: 73).

Caribou Lances

What are presumed to be caribou lance or spear heads come in a variety of materials. All are simple blades, and would have been inserted directly into a shaft or socket, in contrast to the composite, endbladed antler lance heads described above. One specimen is made of bone, with sharp shoulders, a flat, rounded tang, and sharp, parallel lateral margins (Pl. 2,k). It is 143 mm long.

Three others are made of chipped metamorphic stone. One is 86 mm long, and has smooth convex edges tapering to a parallel-sided stem, with a rounded base. Fully 12 mm thick, it still retains patches of cortex (Pl. 2,f). A second specimen is shorter (47 mm), and is clearly unfinished, so that the final outline form is not yet apparent. It has a large untrimmed bulb of percussion near one lateral margin. The third chipped stone example is a broken, rounded base.

A fifth lance blade was cut from sheet metal (Pl. 2,e). It is 88 mm long, and similar in form to the large chipped stone specimen. 2.5 mm thick, it was cut from a heavier grade of metal than the harpoon endblade described above. Like it, however, it has unbevelled, unsharpened edges, and the tang has been pierced for a rivet.

Similar lance heads occur widely, and were normally used to hunt caribou from a kayak (see Murdoch 1892: 243; Jenness 1946: 135). Lance heads used for sea mammal hunting were usually much larger (Murdoch 1892: 241).

Flint-Lock Gun Parts

A sear and broken frizzen spring from a muzzle-loading musket are the only indications of guns at Kugaluk (Pl. 2,h-i). Sears are common to all 19th century muzzle-loaders; frizzens, however, are present only on flintlocks (see Ambler 1960: 266). The frizzen was found with another piece of iron in the hearth in Area B, suggesting that it might have been lost or discarded in the process of being re-worked.

Fishing Gear

Fish Hook Shank

A single antler fish hook shank is an unusually large example of a Class 4 or "Composite" shank (Pl. 2,l) (McGhee 1974: 54). It has an elongated triangular form, an oblong barb hole, and notched lateral margins. Above the mid-point suspension hole, one face has been recessed and flattened for attachment to a separate weight. The opposite face is shallowly grooved for the suspension line. At 132 mm long, this specimen is nearly twice as long as any of the 15 fish hook shanks from Kittigazuit (McGhee 1974: 54-55). Because of its size, it would almost certainly have been used for inconnu.

Similar fish hook shanks appear in most or all Mackenzie Inuit sites (McGhee 1974: 54; Mathiassen 1930: 11; etc.), and in western Alaska, where they may date as early as A.D. 1250 (Giddings 1952: 40).

Fish Hooks

A single fish hook is of European or Euro-Canadian manufacture (Pl. 2,j). It is made of iron or steel, 58.5 mm long, and has an eyed proximal end. It is barbed, and shows the characteristic lateral twist of European-style fish hooks. Unmodified as it is, it could not have been used with a separate shank. It is probably what is referred to in the Hudson's Bay Company accounts as a "cod hook" (HBC, B/157/d/6: 1-5).

Eight straight pins or barbs appear to represent a distinct aboriginal type of fish hook (Pl. 2,m-q). Four are made of bone and four of antler, with lengths ranging from 47.5 to 70 mm. They have a comparatively flat cross-section, a flat, notched proximal end, and taper smoothly to a sharp tip. They would have been lashed to grooved shanks like those collected by MacFarlane from the Anderson River in the 1860s (illustrated in Smith 1984: Fig. 4, d; see also Giddings 1952: Pl. XXIX,19). Similar specimens occur in nearly all Mackenzie Inuit collections, although they have rarely been illustrated or described.

A blank for the production of such hooks was also recovered. It consists of a section of long bone deeply scored for groove-and-splinter production.

Net Gauges

A complete antler net gauge is 166 mm long, with straight sides and a drilled suspension hole (Pl. 3,c). The rectangular gauge section would accommodate a mesh 40 mm wide. A second, broken fragment may be the distal end from a similar gauge. Similar net gauges are found in most recent western Arctic assemblages. Mathiassen (1930: Pl. 4,4) illustrates a nearly identical specimen from Pt. Atkinson.

Net Sinkers

Nineteen irregular flat cobbles have opposite notches indicative of use as net sinkers (Pl. 3,a-b). One very large specimen is only tentatively identified, as the notches may be fortuitous. It measures about 260 x 160 mm, and weighs 1153 g. Other specimens are much smaller, about palm-sized, and weigh from 65 to 390 g. Most have ground notches, although in a few cases they have been unifacially or bifacially chipped. Two examples exhibit crude bifacial chipping around the perimeter, and appear to have combined the functions of net sinker and spall scraper.

Net Floats

A nearly complete bark net float (Pl. 3,d) is of a flat, oval form, 103 x 79 x 31 mm in extent, with a pair of drilled suspension holes at either end. A hole in one face may have held a crystal, like a similar specimen from Holmes Creek (McGhee 1974: Pl. 25,u). A second specimen is badly damaged, but appears similar. "Class 3" floats like these appear at Kittigazuit (McGhee 1974: 57), and elsewhere in the Delta Region.

Fish Spear Prong

What may be the side-prong for a fish spear is 136 mm long (Pl. 3,e). The base is broken, but was evidently thinned and would have been hafted diagonally against the side of the shaft of the spear (cf. Nelson 1983: Pl. LXVII, LXVIII). It has a single barb and is made of antler.

Transportation Gear

Sled Shoes

Twenty-six sled shoe fragments were found, with lengths of up to 315 mm (Pl. 3,h-i). All are made of whale bone, and are about 25 mm wide, with drilled, medially-placed peg holes. Two wooden pegs suitable for attachment were also recovered. Historically, the Mackenzie Inuit used a very short komatik style of sled (Petitot 1970: Pl. 31; see also McGhee 1974: 59).

Swivel Pins

Two broken swivel pins of antler are the only direct evidence of dog traction (Pl. 3,f-g). Complete, they would have been at least 90 mm long. Rare in the western Arctic, swivel pins and other accoutrements of dog traction occasionally appear in late prehistoric and historic contexts in Arctic Alaska (Nelson 1983: 210; Giddings 1952: 59).

Kayak Paddle

A wooden kayak blade was found in the house midden (Fig. 13), but could not be successfully removed because of its large size and poor state of preservation. The piece was about 450 mm long, with the actual blade element being about 350 mm long by 100 mm wide. There was no provision for a bone edging.

Men's Tools and Manufacturing Debris

End-Bladed Knife Handles

One broken specimen represents the handle of an end-bladed knife with an expanded T-shaped butt (Pl. 4,a). It is made of antler, and was formed from at least two pieces spliced and rivetted together at an oblique angle. Two rivet holes are extant, each containing a bone rivet. A second specimen differs in having a much less flared butt (Pl. 4,b), while a third piece, again of antler, seems to be an intermediate wedge from a similar type of knife (Pl. 4,d). It contains a copper rivet in one of its three rivet holes.

T-shaped knife handles seem to be primarily an eastern and central Arctic form (see Jenness 1946: 97 for instance), although an example has been reported from Pt. Atkinson (Mathiassen 1930: 12). Long-handled knives from Kittigazuit differ most obviously in being made from a single piece of antler or whale bone (McGhee 1974: 59).

A second type of endbladed knife is represented by a nearly complete example (Pl. 17,f). The handle consists of a single piece of antler only 74 mm long, with a line of six drilled holes along one margin. One end has been split to hold the iron blade, which is still in place, although badly eroded. It is held with an iron rivet.

Whittling Knife Handles

One complete example has parallel margins, a straight butt, and a plano-convex cross-section (Pl. 4,e). The proximal end has been cut aslant, and has a very shallow blade bed on the flat face. There are two rivet holes, which form the centre of crudely-incised radiating lines on the convex face. The metal blade it would have accommodated would have been

TABLE 2

LOCATION OF TRANSPORTATION GEAR AND MEN'S TOOLS: KUGALUK SITE

Item	Midden	House Fill	F-1	F-2	"A"	"B"	"C"	Cache	Misc.
sled shoes	9	2				4	9		2
swivel pins		1				1			
kayak paddle	1								
endblade knife handles	1					1	1		
knife with iron endblade	1								
whittling knife handles	2								
composite knife handles	4			1		1	1		
misc. handles				1			1		
stone biface					1				
snow shovel (?)				1					
antler pegs		1		1	1	4	5	1	1
whetstones	1	1	1						
burnishing stone							1		
sawed stone		1							
hammerstones	2				3				
lithic debitage	4			11	1		3		2
flattened iron bucket						1			
other metal fragments	8	3	9	17	1	8			

technically somewhere between end and side-hafted, like a modern exacto-knife. The 135 mm long handle is too short to have been braced against the forearm.

A broken and much more problematic specimen appears to be the proximal end of a side-hafted whittling knife (Pl. 4,c). The blade, which must have been of metal, sat in a partial bed/partial slot, and was secured by two iron rivets.

Composite Knives

All but one of seven composite knife handles are complete (Pl. 4,f-h). Each is a rod of antler from 46 to 113 mm long, with a strongly plano-convex cross-section, and a slightly expanded or lipped proximal end. A narrow blade slit has been cut into this end on the flat face, and the handles would have been bound together in pairs, around the blade (see Nelson 1983: 80). One specimen (Pl. 4,f) has an incised grip.

47

Knives like this were used for scoring and etching bone and antler, and were the primary tool used in the production of bone blanks. Their comparative abundance at Ḱugaluk is in keeping with the apparent importance of bone and antler working at the site (see Morrison in press). This is a widespread Inuit tool, specifically adapted to the use of very small iron blades, and is usually displaced by other kinds of knives and saws in situations where iron is more abundant (see, for instance, Murdoch 1892: 155; Jenness 1946: 101).

Miscellaneous Handles

Plate 4,j illustrates the butt end of a wooden handle, with whittled finger grips. It and a smaller antler specimen (Pl. 4,k) could be handles from a variety of tools.

Chipped Stone Blade

A large (80 x 43.5 mm), broken biface is made of good-quality quartzite (Pl. 4,i). The lateral edges are not symmetrical, and the flake scars are large and crude, suggesting that it may be unfinished.

Snow Shovel

A flat spruce board fragment may be part of a snow shovel blade (Pl. 5,a). It has been exfoliated on one face and broken along two edges, and measures 178 x 140 x 8 mm. One edge has a square cross-section and the other appears to be rounded or worn through use. There is no provision for an edge-mounting of bone or antler, a trait shared by snow shovel blades from Kittigazuit (McGhee 1974: 64).

Antler Pegs

Fourteen finished antler pegs were found, with complete examples ranging from 45 to 62 mm long (Pl. 5,d-h). Some of the broken specimens were evidently much smaller, while a single complete ivory peg is 70 mm long. Pegs like these would have been used to join composite tool parts, among other possible functions.

Whetstones

Three river cobbles of fine-grained igneous rock have long, smooth facets resulting from their use as whetstones (Pl. 5,b). More distinctive is a whetstone or burnishing-stone made of fine, slate-like material which has been finished on all surfaces (Pl. 5,c). It has a triangular cross-section and an elongated D-shaped outline, the back of which was produced by sawing through from both faces and then snapping, a difficult technique for such a thick piece (16.5 mm). The other edges are blunt but polished, and one face shows a shallow, polished concave facet. A cruder, broken specimen also shows evidence of sawing and snapping along the back.

Lithic Debitage

Only twenty chert flakes were recovered, ranging in colour from nearly white, through dark red, to the predominant dark grey or black. Eleven measure less than 10 mm in length or width, and appear to be sharpening flakes. Another specimen exhibits shallow unifacial retouch along one edge, while another exhibits extensive cortex. There is also one large slate flake in the collection.

Hammerstones

Five hammerstones show some edge or end battering, and weigh about 500 grams each. Several were found around the Area A hearth, and may have been used for cracking marrow bones.

Metal Debitage

A number of metal fragments were found, indicative of a significant metal industry at the site. For the most part, this industry seems to have concentrated on the reduction of sheet metal, presumably obtained through trade, into tools such as the weapon tips and knife blades already described. Particularly suggestive is a large piece of sheet iron representing nearly half of the side of a metal bucket (Pl. 6,a). It has been flattened, and cut along one end, and probably along the bottom as well, so that its width (120 mm) may not be equal to the original height of the vessel. The uncut end was originally joined to a second side-piece along a rivetted seam. One rivetted handle lug is extant (the other would have been on the other side-piece), and shows very little wear, suggesting not the re-cycling of a worn-out vessel, but the deliberate use of a new one. The original diameter of the vessel would have been about 280 mm, since the side-piece is 420 mm long. This artifact was found in Area B, which appears to have been the most important metal-working area at the site. Nearby was found a finished weapon tip made from similar sheet iron, along with other metal pieces (Table 2).

Several other metal fragments also come from identifiable trade goods, all apparently cut up for re-working. Included is the bowl of a metal spoon (Pl. 6,d), split at the end for hammering flat and with the handle removed, the lower, attachment part of a rivetted copper handle lug for a pot or kettle (Pl. 6,b), the upper part from a similar copper lug (Pl. 6,c), and a flattened, iron kettle spout (Pl. 6,e). More problematic is part of a fairly heavy, bent iron piece (Pl. 6,i), possibly part of a large handle lug, and a thin piece of sheet iron pierced by a row of very shallow, flat rivets (Pl. 6,h). A piece of heavy iron (3 mm thick) has been cut into a parallelogram shape, apparently with a crude chisel (Pl. 6,j). One face has been scored, and the edges of the chisel-mark are slightly melted, indicative of working in a red-hot state. The collection also includes 16 other pieces of cut sheet iron (Pl. 6,l), all less than 50 mm across, one piece of cut sheet copper (Pl. 6,k), about fifteen iron exfoliation scraps (the number grows with handling), and three small copper fragments.

Several items may be of direct native manufacture, although their function is uncertain. Two copper and two iron tubes were found (Pl. 6,f-g), each consisting of a simple one-piece cylinder of sheet metal about 10 mm in diameter, with lengths ranging from 18 to 38 mm. There is also a copper ring with a diameter of about 18 mm; too small to be a finger ring.

X-radiography of ten metal pieces from the site (Laver and Bokman n.d.) suggests that none of this metal comes from tin cans, rather than from the buckets and kettles described. Only one piece gave any evidence of tin plating, and that was questionable.

Women's Tools and Domestic Items

Ulu Blades

Six pieces of ground slate appear to represent the blades of ulus, or women's knives (Pl. 7,a-b). All are too fragmentary to be typed, although at least two do not appear to have been hafted.

Ulu Handles

Two antler handles have been slit for the attachment of an ulu blade (Pl. 7,c-d). Both are unusually narrow (20 mm) as well as quite thin, and were evidently meant for use with metal blades. Both are fragmentary, but one (Pl. 7,c) exhibits two copper blade rivets and seems to have had an upper loop, so that its original form may have been of a hollow D-shape, similar to a specimen from western Alaska illustrated by Nelson (1983: Pl. XLVII, fig. 4).

Needles

Two bone sewing needles were found broken below the eye (Pl. 7,l). Both are flat, and the longer of the two is 75.5 mm long. A much heavier antler needle (Pl. 7,k), also 75.5 mm long, may have been used in cord making or some other comparatively rough purpose.

Needle Cases

A plain bird bone tube 113 mm long may have functioned as a simple needle case (Pl. 7,j). It has been polished smooth, and the cut ends have been nicely ground. Ethnographic Mackenzie Inuit needle cases were normally decorated with large glass beads (see Petitot 1970: 175).

Drinking Tubes

Four much smaller bird bone tubes may have been used as drinking tubes (see Petitot 1970: 186). They too are plain.

Wooden Handle

Plate 7,e illustrates a wooden handle or toggle 84 mm long. It has a round cross-section, and a flat notch has been cut into one face for attachment to a line.

51

TABLE 3

LOCATION OF WOMEN'S TOOLS: KUGALUK SITE

Item	Midden	House Fill	F-1	F-2	"A"	"B"	"C"	Cache	Misc.
ulu blades, slate	2			1		1	2		
ulu handles, antler									2
sewing needles, bone	1						1		
crude antler needle	1								
needle case (?)	1								
drinking tubes	1	1							2
wooden handle/toggle				1					
barking tool	1								
awls	10	2		2	1		7		
antler spoon						1			
marrow spatulas	8	1		4	1			2	1
"fish scalers"	2				1	1			
quartzite scraper	1								
spall scrapers	1	5			2		2		1
cutting board	1								
wooden pegs	1	1					2		
pottery vessel fragments	7	6		1	2		1		1
pottery lamp rim					1				
soapstone vessel rim	1								

Barking Tool

A split caribou metatarsal has been pointed, ground flat, and polished at one end (Pl. 7,m). Nelson (1983: 90, Pl. XXXVIII) illustrates and describes similar tools from western Alaska, used for stripping birch bark from trees.

Awls and Bodkins

Sixteen antler awls or bodkins range from finished bipoints to rough pieces of antler with one end whittled sharp. Six bone examples tend also to be large and crude; one, surprisingly, was made on a rib (caribou?), and at least four others were made on metatarsal blanks.

Spoon

What appears to be an imitation of a European spoon was cut from antler (Pl. 7,i). It is flat, and only 1.5 mm thick.

Marrow Spatulas

Marrow spatulas were particularly abundant at Kugaluk (Pl. 7,f-h), where their manufacture seems to have been something of a local industry. Seventeen were recovered, all made on metatarsal blanks (see Morrison in press). Common to them all is a slightly dished spatulate working end. They otherwise vary a good deal in workmanship and degree of finishing. Only one shows a scalloped hand-grip, while several exhibit the rough, unmodified margins of the original cut blank. Most of the recovered specimens are broken, but would have been up to 300 mm long.

Spatulas like these were used by most recent Inuit to extract marrow from cracked marrow bones.

Fish Scalers

Five modified caribou scapulae seem to have been used as scraping or cleaning tools of some sort. The two most carefully manufactured have had the scapular spine removed, and show signs of use polish along one or both lateral margins (Pl. 8,a). Examples from elsewhere in the western Arctic are usually identified as fish scalers (Giddings 1952: 39-40; Ford 1959: 195; Hall 1971: 33).

Chipped Stone Scraper

A small, chipped bifacial scraper is roughly discoid in shape, and about 31 mm in diameter (Pl. 8,b). It is made of quartzite. Similar scrapers occur at Kittigazuit (McGhee 1974: 67) and elsewhere in the western Eskimo area.

Spall Scrapers

Eleven spall scrapers can be divided into two general categories. All are made on tabular pieces of coarse, basaltic rock, but one group (n=6) exhibits rough bifacial chipping around all or part of the circumference (Pl. 8,c), while the other (n=5) shows only apparent use-wear along the edge of what may have been a natural break (Pl. 8,e). Two examples of the first category have notched edges, suggestive of a dual function as netsinkers.

Cutting Board

A piece from a wooden cutting board exhibits a mass of cut marks on

both faces (Pl. 8,h). The edge has been decorated by a series of paired
incised lines, in a similar fashion to the feather-cutting board described
above.

Wooden Pegs

Four roughly-whittled wooden pegs were found (Pl. 8,d,f-g). They are
49 to 86 mm long, 8 to 15 mm in diameter, and could have been used for a
variety of purposes, including the stretching of small hides.

Pottery

Nineteen pot sherds are typical of Thule and recent Inuit pottery, and
are for the most part coarse, soft, and friable (Pl. 9). Following McGhee
(1974: 72) they can be classed as Barrow Plain Ware. All are undecorated,
and several are coated with burned grease. Temper is abundant and consists
mostly of coarse grit (including mica), and an organic material which appears
to be grass. Thickness ranges from 7 to 15.5 mm. Vessel form is difficult
to determine because of the small size of most sherds, but none shows much
curvature, suggesting comparatively straight-sided vessels. Two rim sherds
(Pl. 9,b,d) have a flat, slightly thickened lip. A third rim (Pl. 9,a) is almost
T-shaped, expanding at right angles both to the interior and the exterior of
the vessel. It probably represents a saucer-shaped lamp.

The collection also includes a modelled ball of unfired clay (Pl. 9,c),
apparently raw material for pottery making, since it includes temper.

Soapstone

A single small soapstone fragment is from the rim of a pot (Pl. 9,e). It
shows the edge of a suspension hole, and appears to represent a typical,
straight-sided vessel.

Soapstone usually appears only in recent contexts in the western
Arctic, and is a trade item from the Coronation Gulf area (Murdoch 1892:
90-93; Ford 1959: 200; McGhee 1974: 71). The evidence from Kugaluk is in
agreement with that from Kittigazuit (McGhee 1974: 71-72), suggesting that
the substitution of soapstone for pottery in the Mackenzie Delta area took
place at a very late date indeed, if at all. Interestingly, 19th and early 20th
century observers, including Stefansson (1914), seem to have been entirely

unaware of the historic use of pottery in the Mackenzie Delta area.

Ornaments

Glass Beads

Seventy-seven glass beads or fragments were recovered from Kugaluk, of which 58 were complete. Following Kidd and Kidd (1970), and Karklins (1985) they can be divided into two main categories on the basis of manufacturing technique. Most are drawn beads, made from a long glass tube or cane, which was cut into lengths which were then ground or polished into the desired shape (see Kidd and Kidd 1970: 48-49). Close inspection with a hand lens reveals longitudinally arranged glass fibers in such specimens. Fifty-two drawn beads or fragments from Kugaluk include 16 which are tubular in form, and 36 which take the form of a slightly flattened sphere, with the length being slightly less than the diameter (still "circular" in Karklin's [1985: 105] terminology). Of the tubular specimens, all but two are of an off-white colour. These two are examples of the comparatively well-known Cornaline d'Aleppo type, with green lining and a red exterior. One of the Cornaline d'Aleppo specimens has a diameter of only 2.9 mm; other tubular beads range in diameter from 3.6 to 5.6 mm. The sub-spherical or "circular" drawn beads are all of a single colour, mostly various shades of blue (33), with two off-white specimens, and one red. Diameters range from 1.6 to 4.2 mm.

Other beads present at Kugaluk are wound, that is they were manufactured by winding the glass fibres around a central wire (see Kidd and Kidd 1970: 49). Twenty-five specimens are all sub-spherical in shape, and are mostly various shades of blue (22). One is purple in colour, another translucent, and one black. Diameters are consistently larger than those of the drawn beads, ranging from 4.5 to 10.5 mm.

The preponderence of blue beads is in keeping with the known preference by Mackenzie Inuit for glass beads of this colour (Bodfish 1936: 210).

Pendants

A moose incisor (Pl. 10,e) and a pathological caribou molar (Pl. 10,d)

LOCATION OF ORNAMENTS AND MISCELLANEOUS ITEMS: KUGALUK SITE

Item	Midden	House Fill	F-1	F-2	"A"	"B"	"C"	Cache	Misc.
beads, drawn, tubular:									
off-white		2		10	2				
red, green-lined				1	1				
drawn, circular:									
blue	1	1	4	19	2	5			
white				2			1		
red					1				
wound, circular:									
blue	1	3	10	2		6			
purple				1					
translucent				1					
black				1					
pendants	3								1
button	1								
placques							2		
toy bow	1								
toy boat			1						
textile			1						

have both been drilled through the root end for suspension. A third pendant consists of a sharpened piece of bone, again drilled for suspension. A section of a bear canine has been polished smooth at the ends, and might also have been worn on a cord through the hollow central cavity.

Button, Placques

An antler button with a sub-rectangular or oval outline has a raised collar on one face, encircling the drilled central attachment hole (Pl. 10,c). Two flat antler placques (Pl. 10,a-b) may have been blanks for the production of similar objects.

MISCELLANEOUS ITEMS

Toy Bow

The nock end of a wooden bow is so small it is certainly a toy (Pl. 10,g). The notches are deeply cut, unlike specimens from Kittigazuit (McGhee 1974: 53). The cross-section is impossible to determine, since the piece has split longitudinally.

Toy Boat

A toy or model boat made of wood is 113.5 mm long (Pl. 10,h). It is bipointed, with a flat bottom and a shallow, gouged depression representing the cockpit. It presumably depicts a kayak.

Textile

A tiny fragment of cloth was recovered from the Floor 1 screen. It measures 15 x 6 mm, and when found showed a trace of red colour, now faded. It might be a section of narrow ribbon.

Unidentified Items

Nineteen flat antler strips exhibit drilled holes, usually about 6 mm in diameter and medially placed. None shows the characteristic use-wear of sled shoes; some may be parts of drying racks, or edge mountings of various sorts. Sixty-two other carved antler pieces or small fragments of worked whale bone represent broken tools and tool-making debitage.

Six broken wood shafts have diameters ranging from 6 to 15 mm. Some have blunt-cut ends, while others show burning and may have functioned at least casually as lamp trimmers. One broken wooden piece shows a zig-zag pattern cut in one margin.

A caribou phalanx was found which had been sawed in two. The proximal half had then been pierced by a gouged hole.

Sixteen cut pieces of birch bark were recovered. None shows any evidence of stitching, suggesting that they may be debitage resulting from the manufacture of bark vessels. Other sorts of raw material include ten pieces of mammoth ivory, and two small, sawed fragments of bear-tooth or walrus ivory. Finally, curiousities possibly picked up for that very reason by the site's inhabitants include a nodule of volcanic conglomerate, two fossil shells, and a piece of fossil coral.

DISCUSSION

The artifacts from Kugaluk compare well with those from other
Mackenzie Inuit sites, including the largest and best described, Kittigazuit
(McGhee 1974). Important similarities include harpoon head and arrowhead
styles, loose harpoon foreshafts, the presence of large antler fish hook
shanks and of netting gear, and the comparative abundance of pottery. At
the same time similarities often extend beyond the Mackenzie Delta region to
include the Western Eskimo in general, or indeed all recent Eskimo from
their Thule culture origin to the modern period. Only two items give an
exotic, eastern Arctic "flavour" to the Kugaluk assemblage; the T-shaped
knife handle and fixed antler lance heads. The former, at least, may be due
to contact with the Copper Inuit, something we know was reasonably
frequent during the 19th century (Jenness 1922:44), and which presumably
had a greater effect on more easterly branches of the Mackenzie Inuit.
Generally, however, the Mackenzie Inuit, or at least the Kittegaryumiut and
Nuvorugmiut branches, appear to share a basic stylistic homogeneity, as
McGhee (1974: 17) has already suggested on the basis of the Pt. Atkinson
material.

The Kugaluk site artifacts can also be used to determine a date for
the site. Inevitably, chronological analysis depends largely on trade goods,
since it is usually these which measure change from the aboriginal,
prehistoric period. The presence of a number of different kinds of objects
have potential dating significance, all of the <u>terminus a quo</u> or <u>terminus ad
quem</u> sort, and none of them very precise.
1. The presence of trade goods, but the absence of such obviously late
material as rifle cartridges, broken china, tin cans, etc. indicate that the
site was occupied sometime between 1800 and the arrival of the American
whaling fleet in 1890.
2. At least two iron pieces from the site appear to come from a flintlock
gun. There is no evidence, however, that the gun was used for anything but
as a source of metal; no gun flints, bullets or bullet moulds, powder
measures, etc., while there is abundant evidence of the bow and arrow.

Firearms were a staple of the Hudson's Bay Company trade in the Northwest throughout most of the 19th century, but as a general matter of Company policy they were not traded to Inuit for fear of violence (see Krech 1979: 107). This policy seems to have been fairly effective until the 1870s, when firearms first appear in regular use among Delta Inuit (Petitot 1970: 153; HBC, B/57/a/4: 7). However, a few guns had been traded into the area at least as early as the 1850s, particularly by Dene trading with Inuit on the Anderson River. As MacFarlane wrote during his first year as factor at Fort Anderson, "...Loucheux also traded a good many furs for Guns, but this must be put a stop to" (HBC, B/6/a/1:4; see also MacFarlane 1891: 35). The scanty evidence of guns at Kugaluk indicates a date after about 1850, and possibly before 1875.

3. All of the bone or antler arrowheads from Kugaluk are self-bladed, yet large, barbed iron endblades appear commonly on ethnographic arrowheads collected by R. M. MacFarlane from the Anderson River in the early or middle 1860s (unpublished material, collections of the Department of Anthropology, Smithsonian Institution). Large iron endblades are clearly an adaptation to a fairly abundant supply of metal, so that the Anderson River arrowheads may be later than those from Kugaluk. The case is far from clear, however, considering the comparatively small size of the Kugaluk collection, and the fact that endbladed arrowheads, being more picturesque, may be over-represented in the MacFarlane collection.

4. It was hoped that the glass beads would prove chronologically sensitive, but unfortunately there is little comparative data available from elsewhere in northwestern Canada. Beads from Kittigazuit seem generally similar to those from Kugaluk, although McGhee (1974: 77) does not distinguish between drawn and wound types. Both collections are dominated by more-or-less spherical blue beads of various sizes. One clear difference is that the Cornaline d'Aleppo beads from Kittigazuit are all brown- or white-lined, while those from Kugaluk are green-lined. Unfortunately, there is no direct chronological control of the Kittigazuit sample, since the site was occupied over the entire 19th century.

Morlan (1972) reports two bead collections from Cadzow Lake, a stratified Loucheux site in the northern Yukon. Level 2, dated to about 1880, produced, again, mainly spherical blue beads of various sizes, but also

a few beads of colours not seen at Kugaluk (or indeed Kittigazuit), especially
translucent beads of pink, red, lavender, green, and white. The Kugaluk
sample does, however, include one clear translucent bead. The Cornaline
d'Aleppo beads from level 2 at Cadzow Lake were green-lined, brown-lined,
and white-lined. Level 3, dated to about 1850, produced only a few beads,
and they were all green- and brown-lined Cornaline d'Aleppos. The Kugaluk
beads are most similar to those from level 2. However, the contrast between
the two levels is not that convincing, considering that the Cadzow level 3
sample is too small to be representative of the variety of beads actually in
circulation at that time. For instance, the Hudson's Bay Company accounts
from Peel's River post (which would have supplied the northern Yukon
through its subsidiary, LaPierre House) list at least six different kinds of
beads in stock in 1854 (HBC, B/157/d/6: 1-5), none of which can be
identified with Cornaline d'Aleppo. With such incomplete and scanty
comparative material, beads are presently of little use in dating historic sites
in the western Arctic.

5. Metal vessels were present at Kugaluk, and were probably used as vessels
as well as sources of sheet metal. MacFarlane (1891: 35) notes "kettles of
sheet iron and copper" on the Anderson River in the late 1850s, and both
"copper kettles" and "tin kettles" appear on Hudson's Bay Company
inventories from Peel's River post from the beginning of the period of Inuit
trade (HBC, B/157/d/6: 1-5, 23-25). In fact they may have already been
widespread by the 1820s (see Franklin 1971: 225).

6. Other Kugaluk trade items, including "cod hooks," also appear on
Hudson's Bay inventories from the early 1850s (HBC, B/157/d/6: 1-5, 23-25),
and again were available earlier through other sources. Franklin (1971: 117),
for instance, describes a Mackenzie Inuk using a "cod hook" as a nose
ornament in 1826.

7. The rivetted seam exhibited by the bucket fragment from Kugaluk is
clearly earlier than the modern lapped and soldered seam. Unfortunately,
little information appears to be available on the date the latter type was
introduced. The production of lapped seams became fully automatic in the
tin-can industry by 1866 (Unglik 1978:32), but this may have little bearing
on the manufacture of larger sheet iron vessels.

8. Traditional native pottery was used and possibly made at the site, yet

none of the early explorers seem aware that the Mackenzie Inuit used anything but soapstone or metal trade vessels. Armstrong (1857: 155), for instance, reports that their cooking utensils were "hollowed out of stone," while Stefansson (1914: 167) writes of his informant Roxy, that "of pottery (he) never saw any." In part the ignorance of early travellers is a reflection of their lack of intimacy with Inuit domestic life, yet the fact that Roxy was unaware of native pottery suggests that it had gone out of use by the 1870s, when he would have been a small child.

Summarizing the above evidence, the Kugaluk site was occupied sometime between about 1850 and 1875. A date of about 1860 seems most in keeping with the available evidence.

CHAPTER FOUR

FAUNAL DIVERSITY AND SEASONALITY

Introduction

The abundance of faunal material from Kugaluk more than compensates
for the relatively modest artifact assemblage. Over 45,000 faunal specimens
were recovered and returned to the Archaeological Survey of Canada for
laboratory identification. The assistance of the Zooarchaeological
Identification Centre, National Museum of Natural Sciences, is also gratefully
acknowledged.

All of the faunal material was first assigned to the general categories
of mammal, fish, and bird (Table 5), of which the mammal category proved
much the largest. Almost three-quarters of the specimens (34,073) could be
further identified to higher taxonomic levels, usually to that of species.
Both MNI ("Minimum Number of Individuals") and NISP ("Number of
Identified Specimens") frequencies were calculated for each taxon. NISP
figures, of course, are simple counts. MNI's were calculated using standard
procedures (Grayson 1984), distinguishing left from right-sided elements, and
mature and immature individuals. In calculating MNIs, the site was
considered as a single analytical unit, rather than as an aggregation of its
constituent areas. This results in lower MNI figures than would otherwise
be the case, but is in keeping with the general structure of the site, which
suggests that none of the site areas can be considered independent. The
consideration of each site area separately, in fact, produces results which
are too complicated to be easily presented, and which moreover are not very
enlightening. Fish bone is an exception. All of the identified fish bone
came from the two house floors, and here it was thought useful to contrast
what may have been two seasonally distinct occupations.

At least 380 individual animals were identified, representing 52 species
(14 mammal, nine fish, and 29 bird). This is a comparatively high figure
(cf. Rick 1980; Balkwill 1987), surely reflecting the ecotonal location of the
site. Despite the considerable range of species, the assemblage is
dominated by caribou, which represent 70.6% of specimens identified above
the class level, and 28.7% of total MNIs.

TABLE 5

NUMBER OF SPECIMENS, BY CLASS: KUGALUK SITE

SITE AREA	MAMMAL	FISH	BIRD	TOTAL	
MIDDEN	14597	1324	543	16464	(35.8%)
HOUSE FILL	2691	893	226	3810	(8.3%)
FLOOR 1	1280	3675	42	4997	(10.9%)
FLOOR 2	2913	8387	75	11375	(24.7%)
AREA "A"	1258	0	96	1354	(2.9%)
AREA "B"	2149	7	49	2205	(4.8%)
AREA "C"	4447	68	24	4539	(9.9%)
CACHE	461	0	0	461	(1.0%)
MISC.	774	1	1	776	(1.7%)
TOTAL	30570	14355	1056	45981	
	(66.5%)	(31.2%)	(2.3%)		

Mammals

Of the 14 mammalian species identified, caribou bone makes up the overwhelming majority, constituting 98.9% of identified specimens and 77.3% of MNIs (Table 6). At least 109 individual animals are present (calculated on right proximal metacarpals), representing, at about 55 kg per animal, a potential meat yield of 5,000 - 6,000 kg. This is much higher than could be calculated for any other taxon. Caribou remains are considered in more detail in the following chapter.

Other mammalian remains are noteworthy by their rarity. Sea mammals are extremely uncommon, and are restricted to beluga, with the possible inclusion of a large seal (presumably bearded seal). All of the sea mammal bone was in the form of ribs or rib fragments, except for one beluga caudal vertebrae, and a scapula fragment. Although beluga are occasionally found in the waters of the Kugaluk estuary, it is suggested that the almost complete absence of remains other than ribs is indicative of their having been killed elsewhere, and the meat transported as rib slabs to the site.

Most of the other mammals are fur bearers, either rodents (muskrat and beaver) or carnivores (black bear, foxes, wolverine, martin and lynx). Included are species characteristic of both the Arctic and, especially, the Subarctic. Frequencies, however, are so low that systematic trapping for commercial trading purposes seems very unlikely. Higher frequencies of fur

TABLE 6

KUGALUK SITE MAMMALS

SPECIES		NISP		MNI	
		f	%	f	%
Rangifer tarandus	caribou	24065	98.94	109	77.30
Alces alces	moose	23	.09	2	1.42
Small beluga/large seal		26	.11		
Delphinapterus leucas	beluga	52	.21	2	1.42
Ondatra zibethicus	muskrat	53	.22	12	8.51
Castor canadensis	beaver	2	.01	1	.71
Microtus cf. eoconomus	tundra vole	3	.01	2	1.42
Spermophilus parryii	ground squirrel	2	.01	1	.71
Ursus americanus	black bear	1	.00	1	.71
Dog/wolf		8	.03		
Canis familiaris	domestic dog	1	.00	1	.71
Fox unident.		11	.05		
Vulpes vulpes	red fox	18	.07	2	1.42
Alopex lagopus	arctic fox	2	.01	1	.71
Martes americana	martin	12	.05	2	1.42
Gulo gulo	wolverine	41	.17	4	2.84
Lynx lynx	lynx	4	.02	1	.71
total		24324	100.00	141	100.01
Unidentified mammal		6246			
TOTAL		30570			

---

bearers, for instance, have been reported from the prehistoric Saunaktuk site on the upper Eskimo Lakes (Balkwill 1987). The low frequency of fur bearers at Kugaluk is especially significant considering that, as we shall see, the site appears to have been occupied into the early winter trapping season. It is unlikely that the paucity of remains is the result of skinning in the field, since in most cases the animals would be frozen, and would have to be thawed, presumably at home, before being skinned out. Moreover, the skins of the two most common fur bearers at the site, wolverine and muskrat, were both used quite extensively in the manufacture of traditional Mackenzie Inuit clothing (Petitot 1970: 171-172), while the basis of the commercial fur trade in the area was overwhelmingly fox (HBC,

64

B/80/d/4: 13).

Canid bones were very rare, and mostly undiagnostic. One complete
cranium, however, can definitely be attributed to domestic dog. It is a
fairly small animal, fitting into the size range of Thule culture dogs
reported from the central Arctic (Morrison 1984).

Fish

Nearly 85% of the over 14,000 fish bones recovered from Kugaluk come
from the two superimposed floors of the excavated house. This is partially a
reflection of different excavation techniques, since only house floor material
was screened and floated, and fish bones are small and otherwise easily
missed. Nonetheless, the high frequency of fish bone in the house is a real
phenomenon, even if exaggerated. House floor material was literally 20% fish
bone by volume, while in other areas of the site it was much more rarely
encountered. Its high frequency on house floors is probably a function of
both consumption patterns and housekeeping activities on the part of the
site's inhabitants, since regardless of taxon, house floor assemblages were
heavily biased in favour of small bone fragments.

Only house floor bone was analyzed in detail (Tables 7 and 8). Of
12,062 specimens, 5395 (45%), most of them ribs, could not be identified
beyond the class level. The remaining 6667 specimens represent at least
nine species, mainly Salmonidae (whitefish, inconnu and trout) and Gadidae
(burbot and saltwater cods). Much the most common is whitefish (_Coregonus
clupeaformis_ and/or _C. nasus_), accounting for almost 75% of fish MNIs.
After caribou they are probably the most important food source represented
at the site.

The size of anatomical elements suggests that most fish averaged about
2-3 kg or less. An exception is a lone inconnu from Floor 2, which may
have weighed as much as 15 kg.

Birds

Although yielding far fewer elements than the fish, birds appear to
have been nearly as important a food source, particularly the waterfowl. A
total of 1056 bird bones represent at least 29 species and 88 individual birds,
most of them comparatively large waterfowl such as swans, geese and large

TABLE 7

KUGALUK SITE FISH: NUMBER OF IDENTIFIED SPECIMENS

SPECIES		NISP FLOOR 1		NISP FLOOR 2		TOTAL	
		f	%	f	%	f	%
Coregonus clupeaformis/whitefish C.nasus		1471	82.4	4077	83.5	5548	83.2
Stenodus leucichthys	inconnu	19	1.1	14	.3	33	.5
Salvelinus namaycush	lake trout	0	0	5	.1	5	.1
Lota lota	burbot	253	14.2	714	14.6	967	14.5
Eleginus gracilis/ Boreogadus saida	saltwater cod	7	.4	6	.1	13	.2
Esox lucius	northern pike	17	1.0	47	1.0	64	1.0
Catostomus catostomus	sucker	18	1.0	19	.4	37	.6
total		1785	100.0	4882	100.0	6667	100.0
Pisces unident.		1890		3505		5395	
TOTAL		3675		8387		12062	

TABLE 8

KUGALUK SITE FISH: MINIMUM NUMBER OF INDIVIDUALS

SPECIES		MNI FLOOR 1		MNI FLOOR 2		TOTAL	
		f	%	f	%	f	%
Coregonus clupeaformis/whitefish C. nasus		23	52.3	90	84.1	113	74.8
Stenodus leucichthys	inconnu	7	15.9	1	.9	8	5.3
Salvelinus namaycush	lake trout	0	0	1	.9	1	.7
Lota lota	burbot	8	18.2	10	9.3	18	11.9
Eleginus gracilis/ Boreogadus saida	saltwater cod	1	2.3	1	.9	2	1.3
Esox lucius	northern pike	2	4.5	2	1.9	4	2.6
Catostomus catostomus	sucker	3	6.8	2	1.9	5	3.3
total		44	100.0	107	100.0	151	100.0

ducks (Table 9). The Kugaluk estuary is an important nesting area for
waterfowl, which are present and abundant from May to September (Martell
et al. 1984: Fig. 5). Year-round residents are largely limited to the
ptarmigans (rock and/or willow), although ravens, snowy owls, falcons and
glaucous gull are also occasional winter residents.

Like the mammals, the avifauna from Kugaluk seems to be a sensitive
index of the ecotonal location of the site, including both boreal forest and
tundra species. Most of the surface-feeding ducks (Anatini), for instance,
are more characteristic of the boreal forest than the tundra, as are the mew
and herring gull, surf scoter, goldeneye, and robin. More strictly arctic are
the tundra swan, white-fronted and snow goose, glaucous gull and common
eider. Only two species appear to be entirely out of their modern range;
the common merganser and trumpeter swan, both of which are now restricted
to more southerly latitudes (Godfrey 1986: 73, 119). However, dense flocks
of common mergansers were reported from the Eskimo Lakes/Liverpool Bay
area in 1974 (Martell et al. 1984: 108), while trumpeter swans are known to
have nested as far north as the arctic coast in the last century (Martell et
al. 1984: 102; Godfrey 1986: 73).

Seasonality

Architectural evidence pertinent to the season or seasons of occupation
at Kugaluk has already been described (Chapter 2), and suggests both warm
and cold-weather occupation. Faunal evidence is more abundant, but also
more ambiguous. Generally, arctic fauna consist either of migratory summer
visitors or year-round residents. There are few if any species whose simple
presence in a site would indicate a winter occupation. Add to this kind of
bias the ease of food storage in an arctic climate, and it is clear that the
association between the season of occupation and the season when an animal
was available or was killed is not a simple one.

Nonetheless, the faunal evidence suggests a picture which is generally
congruent with that presented by the architectural evidence. Certainly there
are a number of warm-weather indicators. Most obvious are the migratory
waterfowl, which are found in the study area only during the May to
September period. The presence of several other species, including
ptarmigan, black bear, beaver and muskrat, may also point weakly to one

TABLE 9

KUGALUK SITE BIRDS

SPECIES		NISP f	NISP %	MNI f	MNI %
Cygnini unident.	swan	21	2.7		
Cygnus columbianus	tundra swan	139	17.6	9	10.2
C. buccinator	trumpeter swan	17	2.1	4	4.5
Anserini unident.	goose	85	10.7		
Anser caerulescens	snow goose	45	5.7	5	5.7
A. albifrons	white-fronted goose	40	5.1	5	5.7
Branta canadensis	Canada goose	35	4.4	5	5.7
B. bernicla	brant	1	.1	1	1.1
Anatinae unident.	duck	110	13.9		
Clangula hyemalis	oldsquaw	59	7.5	9	10.2
Mergus merganser	common merganser	13	1.6	3	3.4
Aythya marila	greater scaup	11	1.4	5	5.7
Anas clypeata	northern shoveler	7	.9	2	2.3
A. acuta	northern pintail	6	.8	1	1.1
Melanitta fusca	white-winged scoter	6	.8	2	2.3
Bucephala clangula	goldeneye	6	.8	3	3.4
Aythya affinis	lesser scaup	4	.5	2	2.3
Melanitta perspicillata	surf scoter	3	.4	2	2.3
Anas crecca	green-winged teal	2	.3	1	1.1
A. platyrhynchos	mallard	2	.3	1	1.1
A. americana	American wigeon	1	.1	1	1.1
Somateria mollissima	common eider	1	.1	1	1.1
Mergus serrator	r. breasted merganser	1	.1	1	1.1
Larus sp.	gull	17	2.1		
L. argentatus/ hyperboreus	herring/glaucous gull	38	4.8	5	5.7
L. canus	mew gull	1	.1	1	1.1
Lagopus sp.	ptarmigan	90	11.4	10	11.4
Gavia cf. stellata	red-throated loon	19	2.4	4	4.5
Grus canadensis	sandhill crane	5	.6	1	1.1
Corvus corax	raven	2	.3	1	1.1
Falco sp.	falcon	2	.3	1	1.1
Nyctea scandiaca	snowy owl	1	.1	1	1.1
Turdus migratorius	robin	1	.1	1	1.1
total		791	100.0	88	100.0
Aves Unident.		265			
TOTAL		1056			

season or another, but since they are non-migratory their value as seasonal indicators is less certain.

As well as presence or absence, changes in the frequency of species may also have seasonal implications. This may be the case when considering fish remains from the two house floors which, on architectural grounds we have already suggested might be seasonally discrete. The lower floor was dominated by whitefish, to the almost complete exclusion of other species. In the upper floor (Floor 1), the frequency of whitefish declines from over 84% of MNI's to 52.3%, with a corresponding rise in the frequency of inconnu (15.9%), and burbot (18.2%). As an abundant fish, and a fall spawner, whitefish are generally the staple of the late summer-fall fishery in the greater Mackenzie Delta area (Martell et al. 1984: 158). Burbot, on the other hand, are among the few fish that spawn under the ice of early winter, when they are apparently most easily caught in nets (Scott and Crossman 1973: 644). Stefansson, wintering with Inuit in the Eskimo Lakes in 1906, noted an increase in the frequency of netted burbot from 10% in the fall to 75% of the catch by December (Stefansson 1962: 359). The increase is not nearly as dramatic at Kugaluk, but the suggestion of two seasonally sequential occupations in House 1 seems to have some support in the faunal data.

The Kugaluk site seems to have been occupied primarily for caribou hunting. As has been noted, caribou are at least minimally present in the site area year-round, but are at their most abundant during the spring migration in late April and early May, and especially during the late summer migration in August and early September. Perhaps the best way of determining the season of death of adult caribou is by examining dental thin-sections (Speiss 1979; Morrison 1983b; Gordon 1984). A sample of 75 teeth from Kugaluk was analyzed by Sterling Presley at the Palaeo-environmental Laboratory, Archaeological Survey of Canada. All were lower right first molars, extracted from mandibles, so that each tooth represents a single individual caribou, with no possibility of duplication. They represent the total of Kugaluk site _in situ_ right mandibular first molars. Each was vacuum-impregnated with resin, thin-sectionned with a slow-speed saw, polished, mounted on a microscopic slide, and viewed under polarized transmitted light with a petrographic microscope.

The teeth of animals which, like caribou, are subject to seasonal
environmental stress contain annular lines similar to the growth lines in
trees. These lines are deposited in two areas of the tooth: in the cementum,
a mineralized tissue around the outside of the tooth below the gum-line; and
the dentine, a similar deposit in the pulp cavity. In the case of caribou
(and most artiodactyls), the dentine is unreadable, so analysis focuses on
the cementum. A control sample of 62 lower first molars from barrenground
caribou with known dates of death had been previously analyzed by the
Palaeoenvironmental Laboratory (Presley 1984). They indicate the deposition
of opaque or dark-coloured cementum during the winter, from December or
January to March, while translucent cementum is deposited during the rest
of the year. By counting annular lines it is possible to accurately determine
the age of the animal at death. By observing the relative thickness and
type of the last annular band it is also possible to determine the season of
death within certain accuracy limits. Generally, readings which are close to
a change from one type of cementum to the other are the most accurate.
For instance, specimens where the opaque annulus was just beginning to
form were consistently found to come from animals which had been killed in
December or (more rarely) January. Readings are less reliable in the case of
animals killed in the middle of the deposition of an annular band, since the
thickness of these bands seems to vary from animal to animal, and from year
to year.

The Kugaluk caribou teeth were read against the control sample. Of
the 75 teeth, eight were too murky or stained to give a clear picture. Most
of these came from immature animals (less than two years old), and it was
consistently found that only adults gave clear readings. Results from the
remaining 67 specimens are presented in Figure 19. Two superimposed
graphs are shown. One gives the month of death as well as could be
determined. The second presents the broader season of death, taking into
account the accuracy limits discussed above. The latter is more reliable, but
the month-of death graph is of course more precise. Both suggest that
caribou consumed and deposited at Kugaluk were killed over about a nine-
month period, beginning in approximately late March (one specimen showing
the beginning of a translucent annulus) and lasting until about late December
(three specimens with the very beginning of the opaque annulus). Summer

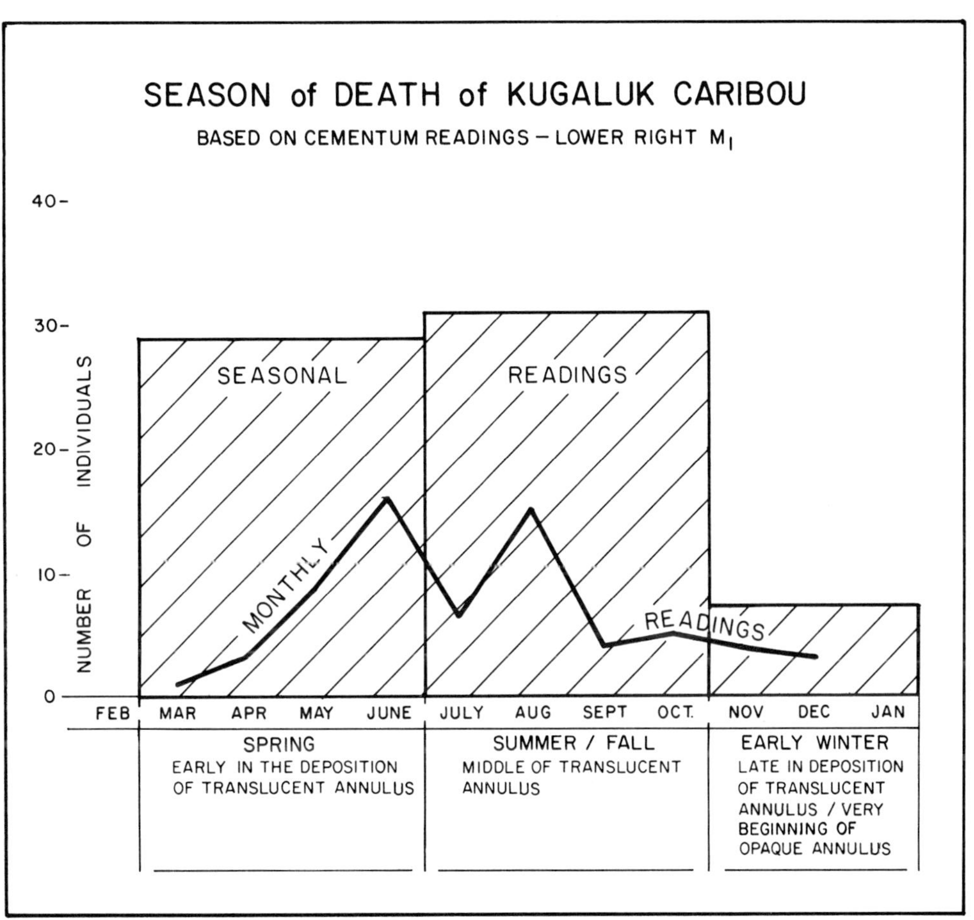

SEASON of DEATH of KUGALUK CARIBOU
BASED ON CEMENTUM READINGS – LOWER RIGHT M_1
NUMBER OF INDIVIDUALS
40-
30-
20-
10-
0
SEASONAL
READINGS
MONTHLY
READINGS
FEB
MAR
APR
MAY
JUNE
JULY
AUG
SEPT
OCT.
NOV
DEC
JAN
SPRING
EARLY IN THE DEPOSITION
OF TRANSLUCENT ANNULUS
SUMMER / FALL
MIDDLE OF TRANSLUCENT
ANNULUS
EARLY WINTER
LATE IN DEPOSITION
OF TRANSLUCENT
ANNULUS / VERY
BEGINNING OF
OPAQUE ANNULUS

appears to have been much the most productive season, from April to October, or perhaps more specifically from May until the end of August. The month-of-death graph shows a bimodal curve, with peaks in June and August. If real, they may correspond with the spring and late summer migrations, respectively, although the spring migration would be over a month late. The season-of-death graph obscures these frequency peaks, and the intervening depressed values for July.

Tooth eruption stages in immature animals are another means of determining seasonality, and fortunately the eruption sequence of barrenground caribou is well known (Miller 1974; see also Speiss 1979: 75-78). Caribou are born in mid to late May, with deciduous premolars and no molars. First mandibular molars appear at the age of 3 to 5 months, i.e. from mid-August to mid-October of their first year. No further cheek teeth erupt over the first winter, but the second molar erupts at 10 to 15 months, from mid-March to mid-August of the second year. The third molar erupts at 15 to 29 months, too long a period to be of use as a seasonal indicator. Finally the permanent premolars come in at 22 to 29 months, from mid-March to mid-September of the third year.

Twenty-one immature left mandibles from Kugaluk were complete enough to be grouped into eruption categories (Figure 20). No foetal or neonatal specimens were represented. Nine exhibit first molar eruption, but none exhibit first molar occlusion with no second molar development. Two specimens exhibit second molar eruption, and eight third molar eruption. Finally, two mandibles show the eruption of the permanent premolars. In other words, two immature animals were killed sometime during the period from mid-March to mid-August (second molar erupting), two more were killed during the largely overlapping period from mid-March to mid-September (premolars erupting), and nine animals were killed sometime in the period from mid-August to mid-October (first molars erupting).

These results are similar but not identical to those obtained from the tooth sections of adult caribou. Both show a generally "summer" kill, although the last immature animal was killed before the end of October, while adults seem to have been killed as late as the end of December. The major difference is the relative importance of the spring/early summer kill, and the late summer/fall kill. The sectioned adult teeth suggest that these

FIGURE 20

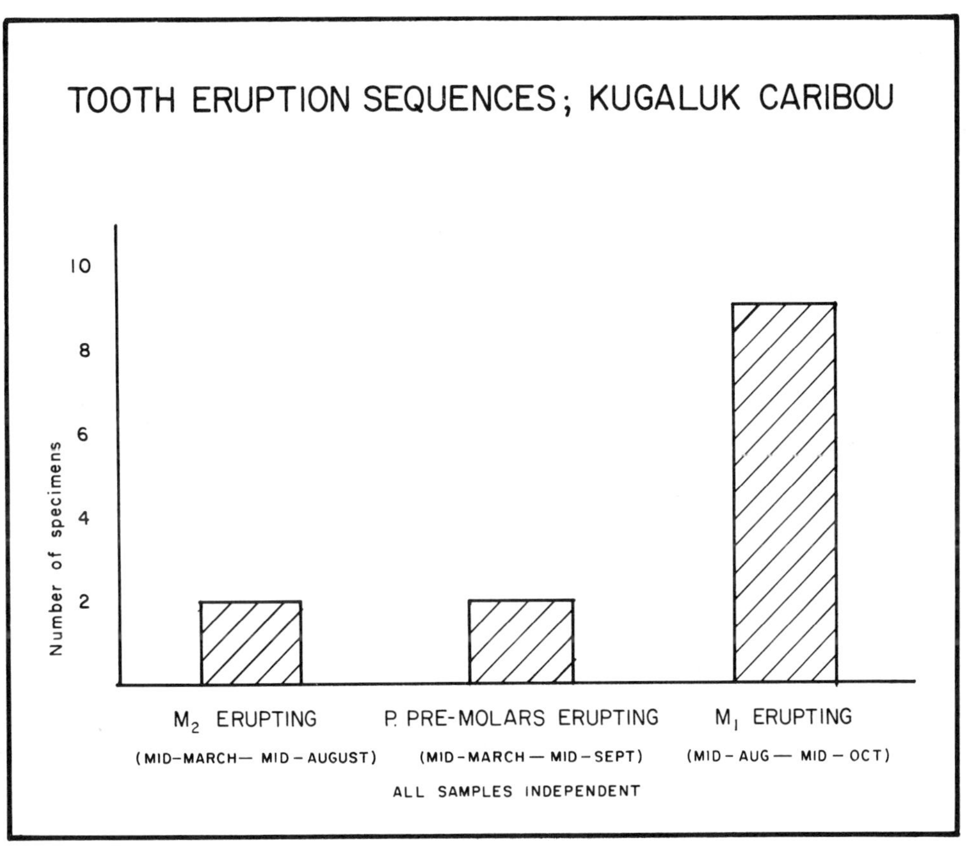

TOOTH ERUPTION SEQUENCES; KUGALUK CARIBOU
Number of specimens
10
8
6
4
2
M_2 ERUPTING
(MID—MARCH— MID — AUGUST)
P. PRE-MOLARS ERUPTING
(MID—MARCH — MID—SEPT)
M_1 ERUPTING
(MID — AUG — MID — OCT)
ALL SAMPLES INDEPENDENT

two periods were of about equal importance, while in the case of immature animals many more were killed during the August to October period than earlier in the year. Possible reasons for this discrepancy include the inherent inaccuracy of one or both methods, selective hunting favouring fall over spring immature animals, and/or simple chance.

Conclusion

Considering both the architectural and faunal evidence, the Kugaluk site suggests that not all Nuvorugmiut spent the crucial August-early September season on the main coast hunting whales. Instead, at least some people evidently engaged in intensive caribou hunting throughout the summer and fall. A simple model of occupation at the site can be suggested, based on the assumption that Kugaluk was occupied only once. This may not have been the case, and the site may actually be a palimpsest of several occupations over a short period of time. But in either event, people (probably three related nuclear families) appear to have arrived at Kugaluk in time for the spring caribou migration in late April. At this time of year the ground is still snow-covered, so they arrived by sled, and would have lived either in snow houses, tents, or some combination of the two. We have no direct evidence of these structures, but they may have been similar to those illustrated by Petitot (see Fig. 21).

It seems clear that the occupation of the site continued through the summer to the time of the August caribou migration. A number of hunting methods were probably employed. Stefansson's (1914: 356) informants recalled both spearing from kayaks and bow hunting in the Kugaluk area. Other economic pursuits appear to have included waterfowl hunting and net fishing.

Sometime during the summer, the three "winter" houses were built and, probably, were used in some fashion, perhaps as some kind of cooking or sleeping structure. Tents, however, would have been the primary form of shelter (see Fig. 22). Fresh meat was kept cold in small cache pits. Other meat, possibly smoked or dried, was stored along with miscellaneous equipment on the large log stage. Much work was done out-of-doors, including cooking and tool-making. In late November or early December, if not earlier, the houses were readied for full-scale occupation, and a new log

74

Mackenzie Inuit spring village (re-drawn from Petitot 1970: Fig. 18)

floor laid in House 1. Some caribou hunting continued, along with net
fishing. There is no positive evidence of occupation after about the end of
December.

Mackenzie Inuit summer camp (redrawn from Petitot 1970: Fig. 19)

CHAPTER FIVE

THE STRUCTURE OF THE CARIBOU BONE ASSEMBLAGE

Introduction

An obvious observation on the caribou bone assemblage from Kugaluk is
that the observed frequency of skeletal parts bears little relationship to the
actual anatomical frequency of these bones in a live animal. For instance,
with an MNI of 109 animals we would expect 2834 ribs, since each caribou
has 26. In fact, only 1075 ribs are represented, 37.9% of the expected figure.
As portrayed in Figure 23, the ratio between observed and expected
frequencies varies from a low of 10.1% (proximal humerus) to a high of 95%
(proximal metacarpal). A figure of 100% is never achieved, since observed
frequencies do not distinguish between left and right sides, or between
immature and adult specimens, and so are slightly lower than the overall MNI
figure, which does so distinguish. Nonetheless, it is clear that the frequency
of anatomical parts varies considerably from what would be expected if the
assemblage were the simple result of the accumulation of complete skeletons.
This chapter considers reasons for the discrepancy.

One means of assessing variations in faunal frequencies is the Minimal
Animal Unit (MAU), proposed by Binford (1978; 1984). The first stage in its
calculation, as with MNI, is the estimation of the Minimum Number of
Elements (MNE) represented by the generally broken fragments in an
archaeological assemblage (see Binford 1984: 50-51). In this study the
criteria (or "counting locations") employed by Klein and Cruz-Uribe (1984:
101-174) have been used. As a measure of anatomical part frequency, the
MAU is then determined by dividing the observed number of elements by
their frequency in a single animal, with the results scaled out of 100. Side
and level of maturity are not considered, as each MAU is used only to
represent itself, not a whole animal, as is the case with MNI calculation.
This means that in an assemblage where observed and expected frequencies
are identical, all MAUs will equal 100. Kugaluk site MAUs are presented in
Table 10.

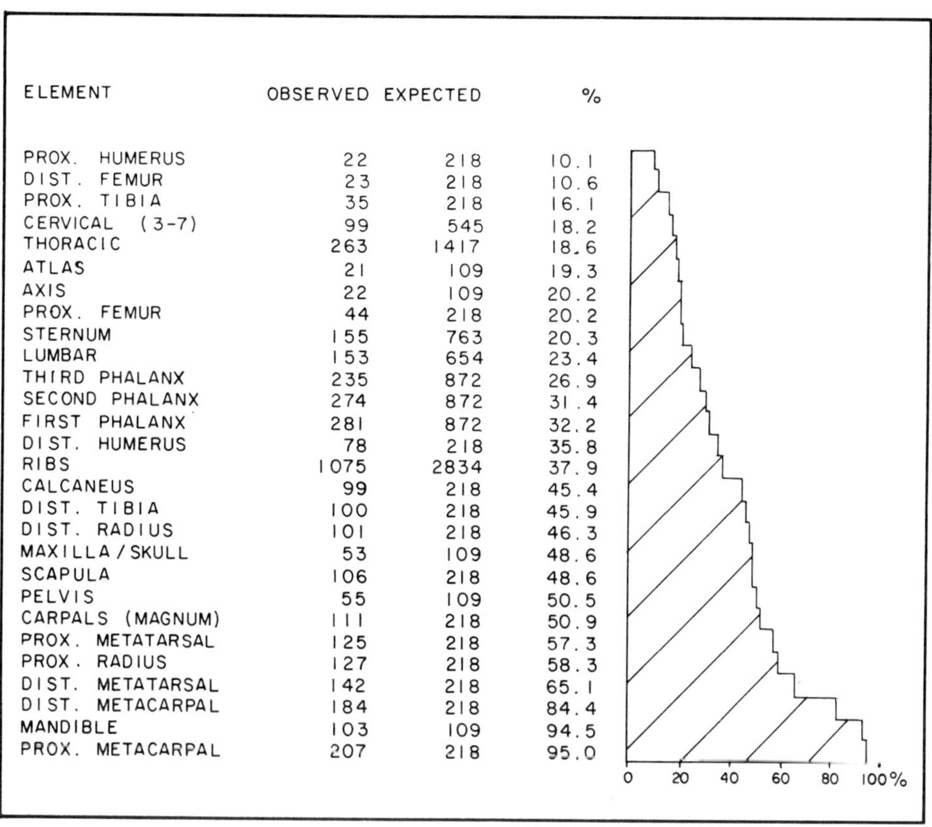

FIGURE 23: Observed vs. Expected Caribou Element Frequencies

Taphonomic and Sampling Considerations

Both taphonomic factors and sampling procedures can effect the
frequency of anatomical parts in a faunal collection. Of the two, sampling
is probably of lesser importance at Kugaluk, although random-sampling
procedures were not used in excavating the site. The goal of excavation
was to explore the various architectural features and activity areas, and not
merely to acquire "representative" faunal and artifact collections. As has
been detailed (Chapter 2), the site was extensively shovel-tested, and
excavation proceeded in areas where concentrations of cultural material were
encountered. These concentrations were quite localized, and the majority of
randomly positioned squares would have produced little or nothing in the way
of faunal or other cultural material. The sample makes up for its lack

TABLE 10

CALCULATION OF KUGALUK SITE MINIMUM ANIMAL UNITS (CARIBOU)

ELEMENT	MNE	N/1	RAW MAU	NORMED MAU
skull (and maxilla)	53	1	53.0	51.2
mandible	103	1	103.0	99.5
atlas	21	1	21.0	20.3
axis	22	1	22.0	21.3
cervical vertebrae	99	5	19.8	19.1
thoracic vertebrae	263	13	20.2	19.5
lumbar vertebrae	153	6	25.5	24.6
pelvis	55	1	55.0	53.1
ribs	1075	26	41.3	39.9
sternum	155	7	22.1	21.4
scapula	106	2	53.0	51.2
humerus-prox	22	2	11.0	10.6
humerus-dist	78	2	39.0	37.7
radius/ulna-prox	127	2	63.5	61.4
radius/ulna-dist	101	2	50.5	48.8
carpals (magnum)	111	2	55.5	53.6
metacarpal-prox	207	2	103.5	100.0
metacarpal-dist	184	2	92.0	88.9
femur-prox	44	2	22.0	21.3
femur-dist	23	2	11.5	11.1
tibia-prox	35	2	17.5	16.9
tibia-dist	100	2	50.0	48.3
tarsals (calcaneus)	99	2	49.5	47.8
metatarsal-prox	125	2	62.5	60.4
metatarsal-dist	142	2	71.0	68.6
first phalanx	281	8	35.1	33.9
second phalanx	274	8	34.2	33.1
third phalanx	235	8	29.4	28.4

of randomness by being quite extensive. In fact, it is virtually complete, except for what might have been found within the two unexcavated houses, and below the tide-line south of the midden.

Selective taphonomic destruction appears to be a much more important factor in producing the faunal assemblage which was recovered. There was no evidence of bones having been removed by fluvial transport, while organic preservation was nearly perfect, as might be expected in a recent site in an Arctic environment. However, there was definite evidence of carnivore scavenging. The Mackenzie Inuit kept dogs (see Petitot 1970: 173), and at least one dog cranium was found in the Kugaluk faunal assemblage. Whether they or their wild cousins are the primary agents responsible is not clear, but definite evidence of canine gnawing was present in most areas of the site. At least 5% of bones show evidence of gnawing in the form of puncture marks, and many of the long bone ends also show signs of furrowing, channelling, and other indications of scavenging (see Binford 1981: 35-86 for a description of these). On the other hand, many quite delicate bones do survive, including the perfectly intact mandibles of very young caribou calves.

Many numeric tests have been proposed to investigate the degree of scavenger destruction in an archaeological fauna. Several proposed by Binford (1981: 176, 219) and used by Speth (1983: 59-61) appear to be quite inappropriate, since they are based on wolf-kill data, and cannot distinguish between natural and cultural agents of bone destruction. One test, for instance, plots long-bone splinters per MNI against shaft cylinders per MNI (Binford 1981: Fig. 4.60). Samples of wolf-kill faunas plotted against these variables display a characteristic V-shape: the number of cylinders rises, and then decreases, as the number of splinters rises. In other words, long bones are gnawed to produce both shaft cylinders and splinters, but as this gnawing continues the cylinders are themselves broken down, resulting in splinters alone. Placing the Kugaluk data into this matrix (Fig. 24), it appears at the far end of the scale, indicating, one would presume, a highly ravaged assemblage.

The difficulty with this test is that it assumes that predator gnawing is the only way in which splinters are produced. In an archaeological site, this is probably not the case, as another test suggested by Binford (1978: Table 9.1) explicitly acknowledges. Here, the observed frequency of splinters is compared with the expected frequency, the latter based on Binford's (1978: 157) study of splinter production during marrow cracking. Where the difference is slight, marrow cracking is presumed to have occurred; where it is greater, additional agents are indicated, including dog gnawing, bone juice production, bone burning, and finally, when very high, bone grease production. Binford (1978: 467) notes that the results do not distinguish between destruction by dogs and either bone burning or bone juice manufacture. Interestingly, Kugaluk shows a difference between

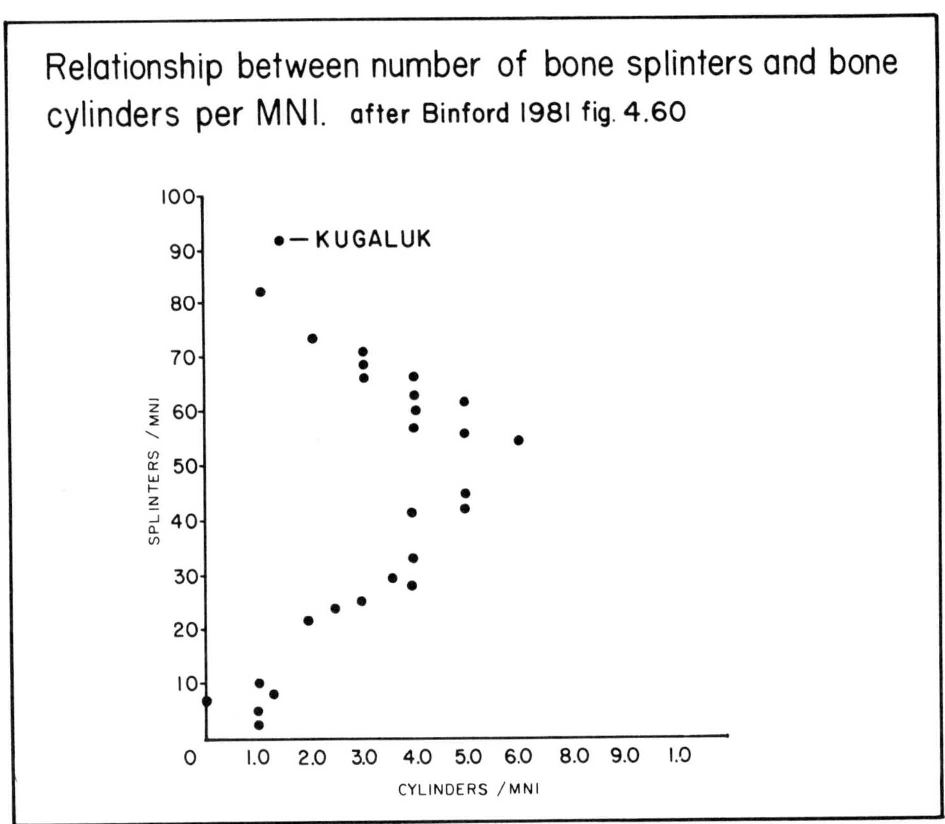

observed and expected frequencies of +5.58 (observed splinters/ articular ends= 9990/1313= 7.54; expected splinters/ articular ends= 2574/1313= 1.96), placing the site in the intermediate category where any of a variety of agents could be responsible. We know that there was considerable bone burning in Area C (see Chapter 2), and that carnivore destruction did occur, but we are no further in numerically assessing the relative importance of each, or in determining their possible effects on the frequencies of faunal elements.

Several other tests based on frequency ratios and wolf-kill data are similar and suffer from the same inability to distinguish cultural from non-cultural factors (Binford 1981: Fig. 4.59, 4.61, 5.07, 5.08; Speth 1983: Fig.

23-25). More promising are survivorship models based on, or related to, bone density. It has been clear since Brain's (1969) Hottentot study that there is a strong relationship between the structural ability of a bone to withstand scavenger gnawing (density), and its frequency in an assemblage which has been subjected to scavenging. A close "fit" between the observed frequency of anatomical parts (MAUs) and their densities would establish the importance of scavenger gnawing as a factor, and go a long way, at least, in explaining the variation between observed and expected faunal frequencies.

Several different density studies have been published. Two examples are Binford's (1981: Table 5.04) Survival Percentage, and Lyman's (1984, 1985: Table 2) Bulk Density. Unfortunately, they apparently do not measure the same thing, since concordance between them using Spearman's Ranked Correlation test (Siegel 1956: 202-213) is significant only at >.05 (Spearman's rho= .2323, N=27). Empirical evaluation of the two models tends to support that of Lyman, in that it correlates much better with observed frequencies at Kugaluk. The relationship between Kugaluk MAU's and Binford's Survival Percentage is significant at <.05, but >.01 (Spearman's rho= .3980, N=27), while the relationship with Lyman's Bulk Density is significant at much less than .01 (Spearman's rho= .7745, N=27) (Fig. 25). This latter correlation appears significant and acceptable. In other words, much of the observed variation in anatomical part frequencies is consistent with selective bone destruction by carnivores.

Utility Indices

It has long been appreciated that more or less conscious cultural or behavioural factors can also be responsible for variation in the frequencies of faunal elements. Almost thirty-five years ago, White (1953: 396-7), for instance, suggested that archaeological faunal frequencies might be influenced by the perceived value of different elements. These elements need not have been introduced in the form of whole animals (or skeletons), but could instead be the products of selective transport after field butchering, with the more "valuable" cuts of meat (and associated bones) being returned to camp, and less valuable cuts abandoned in the field. Complementary "frequency signatures" could thus distinguish habitation sites from hunting camps or kill sites. The latter would produce faunas with high frequencies

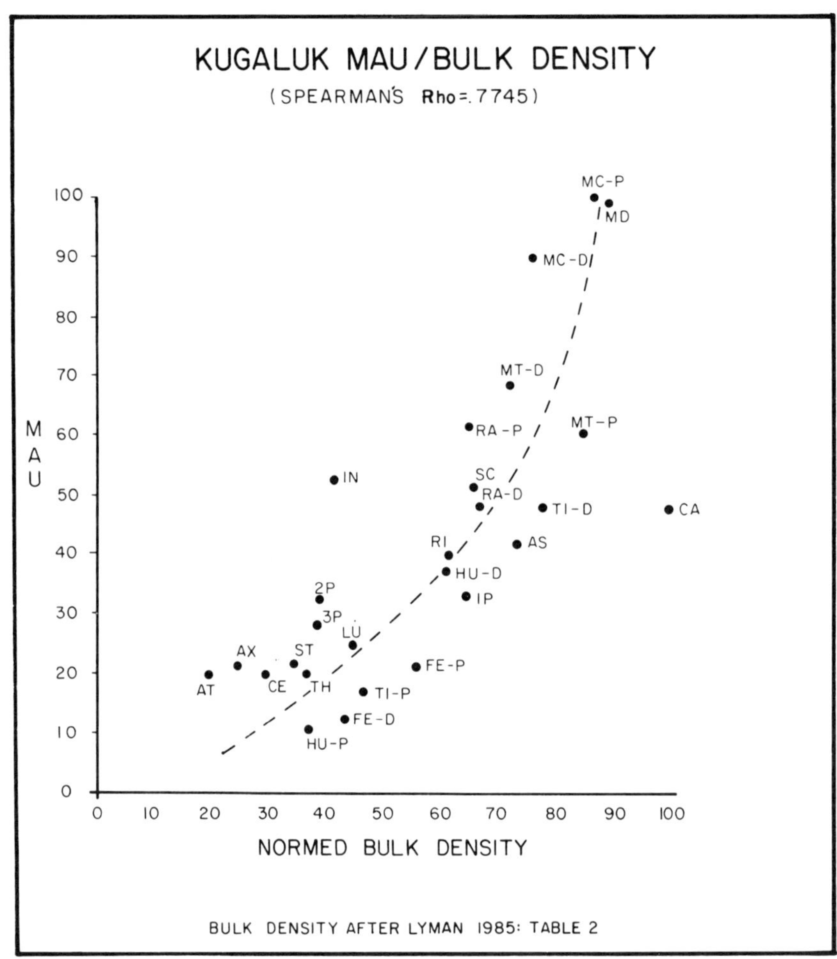

AS=ASTRAGALUS, AT=ATLAS, AX=AXIS, CA=CALCANEUS, CE=CERVICAL
VERT., FE-D=DISTAL FEMUR, FE-P=PROXIMAL FEMUR, HU-DE=DISTAL
HUMERUS, HU-P=PROXIMAL HUMERUS, IN=INNOMINATE (PELVIS),
LU=LUMBAR VERT., MC-D=DISTAL METACARPAL, MC-P=PROXIMAL
METACARPAL, MD=MANDIBLE, MT-D=DISTAL METATARSAL, MT-
P=PROXIMAL METATARSAL, RA-D=DISTAL RADIUS, RA-P=PROXIMAL
RADIUS, RI=RIB, SC=SCAPULA, ST=STERNUM, TH=THORACIC VERT.,
1,2,3P=FIRST, SECOND AND THIRD PHALANX

of "poor quality" elements, and low frequencies of valuable elements, while the reverse would be true of habitation sites.

Indices developed by Binford (1978) operationalize these assumptions by establishing explicit, quantitative scales of value, against which observed frequencies can be compared. These indices result from Binford's study of Nunamiut caribou hunting and processing strategies in north Alaska. "Value" is perceived solely in terms of nutritional value; the meat, marrow, and bone grease represented by each element, considered along with the proportion of unusable bone or sinew. Three indices result; a Meat Utility Index, a Marrow Index, and a White Grease Index, each scaled out of 100. These values were then combined into a General Utility Index for each element of the caribou skeleton. Since certain low-utility elements may be attached as riders to higher utility elements, this index was in turn adjusted to produce a Modified General Utility Index, known as an MGUI. The various utility indices are presented in Table 11, along with Kugaluk site MAUs.

To a great extent Binford's utility indices are based on the observed "facts" of caribou anatomy. Unfortunately, they are the "facts" of only a single caribou; a young, adult male in good condition. We as yet have no grasp on the range of individual or seasonal variation. The nutritional state of caribou, and consequently their food value to a hunter, varies throughout the year, with the two sexes following different calendars. During the spring and early summer, gravid and lactating females are in very poor nutritional shape, while after the fall rut the males are very thin, and the cows prime. All of this would have little or no effect on the relative utility of various parts if nutritional state had a constant effect on all anatomical parts, raising or lowering their food value uniformly. This is certainly not the case, and many parts which are of comparatively high utility in an animal in good condition are simply worthless if the animal is in poor condition (see Binford 1978: 40).

The utility indices, then, present an idealized, static picture of the nutritional value of caribou. Moreover, this picture is probably all that the archaeological data will accommodate, since it is doubtful that sexual and seasonal characteristics can ever be adequately controlled in most faunal samples. Speth's (1983) excellent analysis of the Garnsey bison fauna is very much facilitated by his ability to accurately sex many bison elements,

TABLE 11

KUGALUK SITE MAUs AND THE UTILITY INDICES

ELEMENT	MAU	MEAT INDEX	MARROW INDEX	GREASE INDEX	MGUI
skull (and maxilla)	51.2	9.1	1.0	1.0	8.7
mandible	99.5	31.1	5.7	1.0	30.3
atlas	20.3	10.1	1.0	1.0	9.8
axis	21.3	10.1	1.0	1.0	9.8
cervical vertebrae	19.1	37.0	1.0	1.0	35.7
thoracic vertebrae	19.5	47.2	1.0	1.0	45.5
lumbar vertebrae	24.6	33.2	1.0	1.0	32.0
pelvis	53.1	49.3	7.8	1.0	47.9
ribs	39.9	51.6	1.0	1.0	49.8
sternum	21.4	66.5	1.0	1.0	64.1
scapula	51.2	44.7	6.4	7.7	43.5
humerus-prox	10.6	28.9	29.7	75.5	43.5
humerus-dist	37.7	28.9	28.3	27.8	36.5
radius/ulna-prox	61.4	14.7	43.6	37.6	26.6
radius/ulna-dist	48.8	14.7	66.1	32.7	23.0
carpals (magnum)	53.6	–	1.0	36.5	15.5
metacarpal-prox	100.0	5.2	61.7	16.7	12.2
metacarpal-dist	88.9	5.2	67.1	42.5	10.5
femur-prox	21.3	100.0	33.5	26.9	100.0
femur-dist	11.1	100.0	49.4	100.0	100.0
tibia-prox	16.9	25.5	43.8	69.4	64.7
tibia-dist	48.3	25.5	92.9	26.1	47.1
tarsals (calcaneus)	47.8	–	–	29.9	31.7
metatarsal-prox	60.4	11.2	81.7	17.9	29.9
metatarsal-dist	68.6	11.2	100.0	43.1	23.9
phalanges (p.1)	33.9	1.7	1.0	23.9	13.7

and by the fact that the procurement of bison took place over a very brief
period in their nutritional cycle. Sexual dimorphism is much less marked in
caribou (see Speiss 1979: 82–86), so that very few elements can be accurately
sexed and, as we have already seen, the Kugaluk site seems to have been
occupied over a period of many months. Any exploration of the
relationship between utility and frequency will have to be a general one,
obscuring potentially important seasonal changes in the utilization of
different elements.

Figure 26 graphically portrays the relationship between Kugaluk site
faunal frequencies (MAUs) and the Modified General Utility Index, while

Figure 27 portrays the same relationship concentrating only on limb elements. Table 12 shows the Spearman's Ranked Correlation Coefficients between MAUs and all four utility indices, calculated for both the total anatomical complement, and again for limb elements alone. The decision to consider the limb elements separately as well as with the rest of the skeleton is made following Speth (1983: Table 14), and yields useful results.

Several observations can be made. Firstly, none of the correlations is as strong as that with Bulk Density, suggesting that scavenger destruction was the most important, or at least the ultimate, agent responsible for the composition of the caribou assemblage. In other words, carnivore destruction either occurred after cultural selection, or it had a greater impact on the assemblage, or both. Of the various utility indices, the MGUI and Meat Utility Index, in that order, appear to be the best predictors of anatomical part frequencies at Kugaluk. Both produce "good" negative correlations, significant at $<.05$ when considering the total anatomical complement, and at $<.01$ for limb elements alone. The fact that correlations are negative indicates that the assemblage is skewed in favour of the less valuable elements, with value measured in terms of overall utility and meat. The Marrow and White Grease Indices yield much poorer results, with probabilities consistently greater than .05. The Marrow Index correlations are at least unique in being positive. However, because the Marrow Index is in turn positively correlated with Bulk Density (Lyman 1985: Table 3), it is probable that the MAU/Marrow Index relationship has been distorted in a positive direction by the effects of carnivore ravaging. This is borne out by applying a "correction factor" to the MAU calculations (see Binford 1981: 224), the results of which decrease the relationship almost to the point of randomness (Spearman's Rho= +.1267, N=23). This same correction has little effect on other utility index correlations.

Results such as these are strikingly similar to those reported by Speth (1983: Table 14) from the Garnsey bison kill site. Negative utility correlations coming from what is otherwise a habitation site suggest that Kugaluk functioned as a residential hunting camp, where a food surplus was produced and removed from the site as part of the seasonal subsistence round. A reading of Stefansson's (1914: 356) account might suggest that this surplus was returned to Nuvurak or one of the other large coastal villages

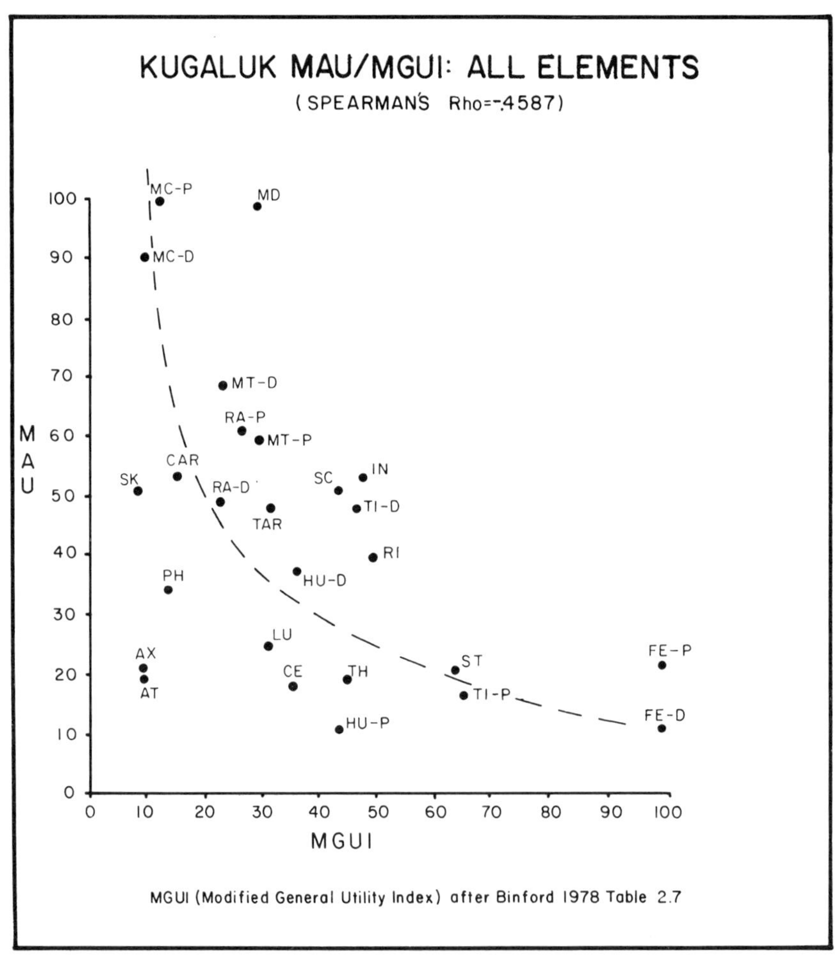

KUGALUK MAU/MGUI: ALL ELEMENTS
(SPEARMAN'S Rho=-.4587)
100
90
80
70
60
50
40
30
20
10
0
M
A
U
MC-P
MD
MC-D
MT-D
RA-P
MT-P
CAR
SC
IN
SK
RA-D
TI-D
TAR
RI
PH
HU-D
LU
AX
ST
FE-P
CE
TH
AT
TI-P
HU-P
FE-D
0 10 20 30 40 50 60 70 80 90 100
MGUI
MGUI (Modified General Utility Index) after Binford 1978 Table 2.7

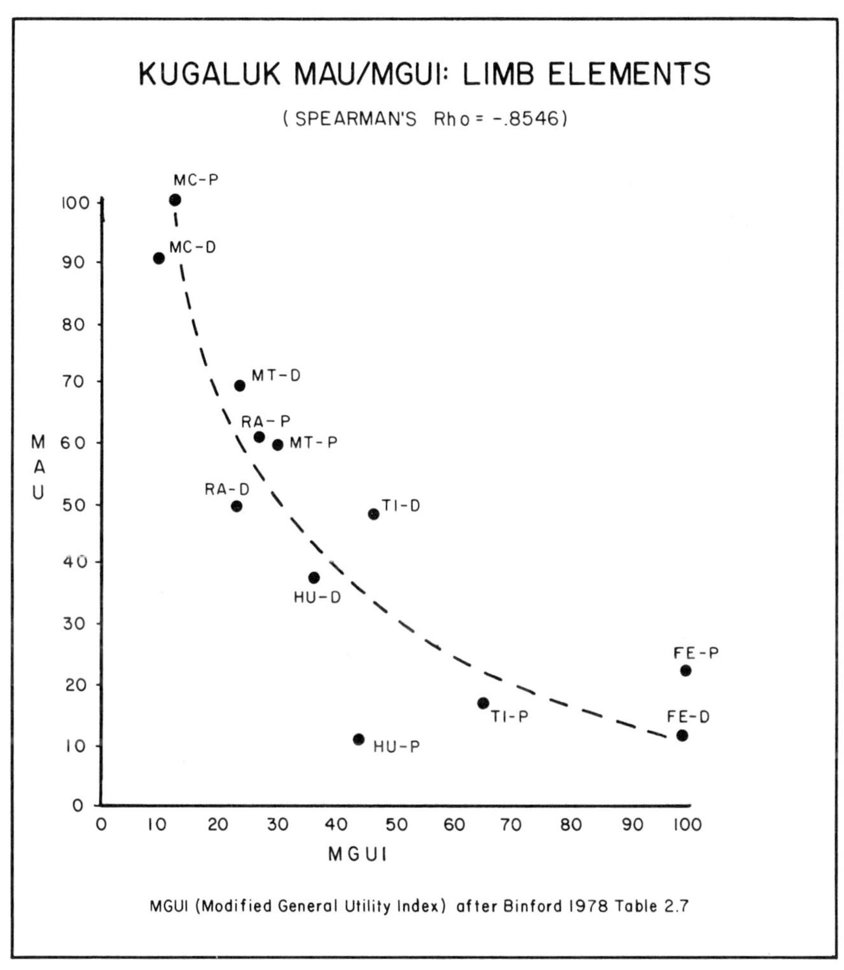

KUGALUK MAU/MGUI: LIMB ELEMENTS
(SPEARMAN'S Rho = -.8546)
MAU
MGUI
MC-P
MC-D
MT-D
RA-P
MT-P
RA-D
TI-D
HU-D
FE-P
TI-P
FE-D
HU-P
100
90
80
70
60
50
40
30
20
10
0
0 10 20 30 40 50 60 70 80 90 100
MGUI (Modified General Utility Index) after Binford 1978 Table 2.7

TABLE 12

SPEARMAN'S RANKED CORRELATIONS
MAU's and Utility Indices

		Rho	N	P
TOTAL MAU	/MGUI	−.4587	26	<.05
LIMB MAU	/MGUI	−.8546	12	<.01
TOTAL MAU	/MEAT INDEX	−.4017	24	<.05
LIMB MAU	/MEAT INDEX	−.9046	12	<.01
TOTAL MAU	/MARROW INDEX	+.3542	23	>.05
LIMB MAU	/MARROW INDEX	+.5594	12	>.05
TOTAL MAU	/GREASE INDEX	+.0028	26	>.05
LIMB MAU	/GREASE INDEX	−.5035	12	>.05

All tests one-tailed

for winter consumption. However, it is also possible that the surplus was cached in some convenient spot, to be retrieved when people returned inland in the spring. This is what MacFarlane (1905: 681) reports the Avvaqmiut of the Anderson River did. In any event, since the surplus was not eaten on the spot, it seems very unlikely that Kugaluk was occupied much beyond the end of the caribou-hunting season in December. The fact that limb bone correlations seem to be stronger than those from the entire anatomical complement suggests that they exported mostly limb elements.

CHAPTER SIX

DISCUSSION AND CONCLUSIONS

The interpretation of the Kugaluk site forms the basis of several important observations on the culture and subsistence practices of the mid-nineteenth century Nuvorugmiut. The site was occupied sometime between about 1850 and 1875, most probably about 1860. It seems to represent a group of people still largely aloof from the fur trade, yet nonetheless with some real access to European trade goods, either directly or indirectly. The site may be contemporaneous with the brief florescence of Fort Anderson, and with Peel's River post's first call for another assistant to help with the Inuit trade. Yet the people who lived at Kugaluk seem to have ignored the June trading season, and apparently had scant interest in commercial trapping, even though the site was occupied during the early winter trapping season. They had some trade goods, chiefly metal, and glass beads, but the traditional material culture was still largely intact. They presumably spent the late winter and early spring on the main coast, hunting seals. They certainly spent most of the rest of the year in the intensive hunting of caribou.

If the way of life represented at Kugaluk seems essentially aboriginal, at the same time it does not differ radically from that described by Stefansson's informants, recalling the 1880s and '90s (Stefansson 1914). Of course, by this time major changes had occurred, but Stefansson was chiefly interested in the traditional culture, and does not dwell on obvious examples of acculturation. The important point is that the kind of intensive spring through fall inland caribou hunting described by Stefansson does not appear to have been the product of cultural change and devolution, but pre-dates the demise of whaling, and probably the fur trade. It would appear that the man who told Richardson in 1848 that the Nuvorugmiut spent August and early September whaling (Richardson 1851: 257) was speaking only of his own immediate group.

Evidently, not all Nuvorugmiut followed the same seasonal round, especially during the crucial August-early September period, when the whaling and caribou-hunting seasons conflict. It is impossible to estimate what percentage of Nuvorugmiut followed one course or the other, but it may be that their motives and positions in life were essentially different. Caribou are a reliable and valuable resource, supplying both meat and, especially, the hides so necessary for clothing and trade. Open-water whaling is less reliable, but more spectacular. When successful, it yields vast quantities of meat, baleen, and above all, prestige.

We have almost no direct information on Nuvorugmiut social organization or the role which whaling may have played in it. However, comparative information is available for better known and closely related groups, including other Mackenzie Inuit, and especially the Northwest Alaskan Inupiat. As described by Burch (1980), the Inupiat were divided into 25 "societies" at contact, occupying territory from the Seward Peninsula to the mouth of the Colville River. Each was a named, land-holding group, recognized as such by itself and by other, comparable groups. Each was made up of several independent, bilaterally extended "local families," which might number as many as 50 or 100 people. The local family was the basic political unit, with its own leader, so that group cohesion at the society level was weak except in the face of an external threat. In the course of a normal year, most or all societal members would meet face-to-face, however, and marriage and kinship were important ties binding local families. As Burch (1980: 263) puts it, "A Northwest Alaskan Eskimo society is ... most easily conceived of as a network in which the nodes were extended families, and the lines between the families were less active or temporarily inactive kinship ties of various kinds.... The outer boundary of the system was defined by a relatively sharp break in this network of relationships."

The social organization of the Central Eskimo to the east was significantly different, if only because scarce resources meant that population densities were too low to sustain the degree of interaction characteristic of a Northwest Alaskan society. The social entity most comparable in size to the Alaskan society was, in the Central Arctic, the "tribe"; a maximal social grouping such as the "Copper Inuit" or "Netsilik." These units, however, occupied territories which were much larger; about 200,000 square-kilometers for the Copper Inuit, for instance, as compared with about 20,000 for a North Alaskan society. As such, a Central Eskimo

"tribe" was not (and could not be) a self-perceiving entity, but is instead
an abstraction, isolated and named by social anthropologists, mainly on
linguistic grounds (see Damas 1968: 146). The five Mackenzie Inuit "-miuts"
resemble Alaskan societies, not merely in terms of population density and
territorial size, but in other ways as well, including the presence of the
important institutions of umialik (Stefansson 1914: 164) and karigi (Franklin
1971: 217; Stefansson 1914: 170). Like the Northwest Alaskan Inupiat, they
were Western Eskimo.

The Western Eskimo local family was centred on the umialik. The
term literally means "boat owner," referring specifically to the large skin
umiak. A better, less literal translation would be "rich man," "boss," or
"underwriter," depending on the context in which it was used, for not all
umialik owned boats, and not all boat-owners were umialik (Burch 1980: 296;
see also Lowe 1984: 69). Western Eskimo societies were stratified, and
people of the same sex and equivalent age status did not have equal access
to the basic resources of life. As the head of a large local family, the
umialik served as a focus of redistribution, and with his immediate relatives
had more food, more trade goods, and more power than anyone else. At
the other end of the hierarchy were people who were little better than
slaves, usually orphans or genealogically isolated individuals (Burch 1980:
265). Among the Mackenzie Inuit, the term for such people was ilialuk
(Stefansson 1914: 164), at Pt. Barrow iilyaaruk (Spencer 1959: 153).

Inevitably, not all local families were of equal size and power. The
more powerful families tended to have their winter houses at the most
advantageous locations, while weaker groups were forced into more marginal
areas of the societal territory (cf. Richardson 1851: 269). Several local
families might be represented at large, central villages. Here, each well-
organized local family would normally have its own karigi or ceremonial
house. These were a focus of family identity and a location for ceremonial
functions, and were used for dancing and the repair and construction of
tools (Burch 1980: 271). Sometimes they are described as "men's houses,"
although women were not barred, and men normally ate and slept at home.
Among the Mackenzie Inuit they were used primarily in the summer and
fall, at the time of the whale hunt (Stefansson 1914: 136). There was at
least one at Nuvurak (Franklin 1971: 217), and three at Kittigazuit

(Stefansson 1914: 170).

There was a direct relationship between the size and power of a local family and the effectiveness of its umialik. The more successful an umialik the larger his local family became, as more people were tempted to affiliate with it. Because families were bilateral and largely exogamous, a "well-connected" individual had considerable choice about which kinship ties to activate, and which to ignore. By the same token, a successful umialik was not merely someone who was shrewd and personally competent, but also one who had a large potential backing; a man with many relatives (Burch 1980: 265). The office, then, may have had some hereditary tendency (see Spencer 1959: 179), which may account for references to patrilineal "chiefs" among the Mackenzie Inuit (Petitot 1970: 191). As Stefansson (1914: 172) puts it "...when a chief died his eldest son became chief; if he had no son, his brother became chief; if no brother, some relative in whom the people had confidence." An unsuccessful umialik would lose his following and, if sufficiently disliked, could even be assassinated (Burch 1980: 265). Apparently, a violent "coup" of this sort occurred at Kittigazuit in the late 1880s (McGhee 1986).

On a conceptual level, the office of umialik was closely linked with bowhead whaling. The umialik was the captain of a hunting group, and as a "boat-owner", this was typically a whaling crew (Spencer 1959: 152). The karigi was to a large extent organized around him, and it will be recalled that the karigi at Nuvurak was surrounded by the skulls of 21 bowhead whales. One large house there was also decorated with the skulls of three or four whales (Franklin 1971: 217), and presumably belonged to an important umialik. Not all Western Eskimos hunted bowheads, and not all umialik were whalers. But where whaling was practised, the role of whaling captain was central to the prestige of the umialik, and provided the basis of the food surplus he commanded (Spencer 1959: 180). According to Stefansson (1914: 168), among the Mackenzie Inuit "the man who steers the boat is 'umialik'".

There may have been some differences between Mackenzie Inuit and North Alaskan whaling. In particular, women rowers were sometimes used in the Mackenzie region (Stefansson 1914: 168), a practice rarely necessary in Alaska. M'Clure writes of the hunt at Cape Bathurst:

An Oomaiak, or women's boat, is manned by ladies,
having as harpooner a chosen man of the tribe; and a
shoal of small fry, in the form of Kyaks (sic), or
single-man canoes, are in attendance. The harpooner
singles out a fish, and drives into its flesh this
weapon, to which an inflated seal-skin is attached by
means of a walrus-hide thong. The wounded fish is
then incessantly harassed by the men in the kyaks
with weapons of a similar description, a number of
which, when attached to the whale, baffle its efforts
to escape, and wear out its strength, until in the
course of a day, the whale dies from sheer exhaustion
and loss of blood (M'Clure 1969: 93).

According to M'Clure (1969: 93), a successful hunt was celebrated with
"great orgies," the hero of which was the harpooner, who was rewarded
with a tattoo. He may be mistaken, for he makes no reference to the
steersman, who as we have seen was normally the _umialik_, and hence the
more likely or usual recipient of such honours. Thus Stefansson's
(1914:168) informant Roxy identified the steersman as _umialik_, describing
the case of his own father, chief at Kopuk.

Roxy tells that when a man of his village killed a
whale (as boat-steerer) he wore a crowskin with
beaks and claws across his back for some time after.
It was also usual to tattoo him with two lines running
from the corners of the mouth to the angle of the
lower jaw.... His father killed a whale about in
October and wore a crowskin until about April. When
the houses had all been fixed and all preparations made
for winter, he sent word out that there would be
eating and ula-hula at his house for he intended
tattooing because of the whale he had killed.

Petitot (1981:113) records that successful whalers at Cape Bathurst
were rewarded with a tattooed cross on the shoulder. One old Avvaqmiut

who Petitot talked with had three such crosses on one shoulder and four on the other. "These, he said, "are glorious marks. They commemorate whales that I killed and brought ashore on the coast" (Petitot 1981: 113). This man, "white-haired old Kroanark," was the older brother of Noulloumallok-Innonarana, the most important chief of the Avvaqmiut (Petitot 1970: 138). In his prime he, too, had evidently been an umialik of importance.

Considering the prestige implications of whaling and the nature of Western Eskimo society, it is unlikely that the people who occupied the Kugaluk site during the caribou season were of the status or immediate family of a Kroanark or a Noulloumallok-Innonarana. They would have been people of no particular status, not necessarily ilialuk, but members of a comparatively small local family. The Tuktoyaktuk Peninsula has few promontories suitable for whaling, and what whaling did take place was probably not reliable enough to be the sole support of the entire social group. It was an option that was probably not open to all. The inhabitants of Kugaluk had access to thousands of kilograms of caribou meat, and hundreds of kilograms of fish. They had hides to trade, and a stable resource to exploit, but they would not have had the prestige or backing to spend their summers on the main coast in the glorious pursuit of baleen whales.

The fact that the Nuvorugmiut abandoned whaling prior to the arrival of the American whaling fleet is one indication of its real subsistence importance. By the mid 1880s, they had suffered several infectious disease epidemics and other forms of social disruption, including the continuing disruption of traditional territorial boundaries. It seems likely that the web of kinship ties and obligations upon which the powerful umialik families depended broke down, and there was not sufficient motivation to re-formulate them. As overall population declined and the fabric of society unravelled, people chose to abandon an economic pursuit which had been more concerned with the acquisition and maintenance of status than with "bare bones" economics. Perhaps even more importantly, different status roles were appearing in a more and more white-dominated economy, and powerful men derived their status from pursuits more reliable than open-water whaling. Where it had once been only half of a dual economic system, the inland caribou-oriented strategy we see at Kugaluk eventually

became the only economic basis of the Nuvorugmiut in the generation prior
to their final destruction.

REFERENCES CITED

AMBER, JOHN T (ed.). 1960. Gun Digest, 14th edition. Gun Digest: Chicago.

ARMSTRONG, ALEXANDER. 1857. A Personal Narrative of the Discovery of the North-West Passage. Hurst and Blackett: London.

ARNOLD, CHARLES. 1986a. A nineteenth-century Mackenzie Inuit site near Inuvik, Northwest Territories. Arctic 39(1): 8-14.

ARNOLD, CHARLES. 1986b. Archaeological investigations in the Mackenzie Delta and Eskimo Lakes, 1985. MS 2495, on file with the Archaeological Survey of Canada, Canadian Museum of Civilization, Ottawa. 99 pp.

ARNOLD, CHARLES. 1987. Preliminary report on 1986 activities of the Mackenzie Delta Heritage Project: excavations at Gupuk (NiTs-1). MS 2821, on file with the Archaeological Survey of Canada, Canadian Museum of Civilization, Ottawa. 34 pp.

BALKWILL, DARLENE. 1987. An arctic cornucopia: faunal diversity at the Saunaktuk site, NWT. Paper presented to the Annual Meeting of the Canadian Archaeological Association, Calgary.

BANFIELD, A.W.F. 1974. The Mammals of Canada. University of Toronto Press: Toronto.

BINFORD, LEWIS. 1978. Nunamiut Ethnoarchaeology. Academic Press: New York.

BINFORD, LEWIS. 1981. Bones: Ancient Men and Modern Myths. Academic Press: New York.

BINFORD, LEWIS. 1984. Faunal Remains from Klasies River Mouth. Academic Press: New York.

BOCKSTOCE, JOHN. 1986. Whales, Ice, and Men: The History of Whaling in the Western Arctic. University of Washington Press: Seattle.

BODFISH, HARTSON. 1936. Chasing the Bowhead. Harvard University Press: Cambridge.

BRAIN, C.K. 1969. The contribution of Namib Desert Hottentots to an understanding of australopithecine bone accumulations. Scientific Papers of the Namib Desert Research Station 39: 13-22.

BURCH, ERNEST S. 1976. The "Nunamiut" Concept and the Standardization of Error. In, Contributions to Anthropology: The Interior Peoples of Northern Alaska, Edwin Hall, ed., pp. 52-97. National Museum of Man Mercury Series, Archaeological Survey of Canada Paper 49.

BURCH, ERNEST S. 1980. Traditional Eskimo Societies in Northwest Alaska. In, Alaskan Native Culture and History, Y. Kotani and W. Workman, eds. Senri Ethnological Series 4: 253-304.

BURCH, ERNEST S. 1981. The Traditional Eskimo Hunters of Point Hope, Alaska: 1800-1875. North Slope Borough, Barrow.

DAMAS, DAVID. 1968. The Eskimo. In, Science, History and Hudson Bay, C.S. Beals, ed., pp. 141-171. Dept. of Energy, Mines and Resources: Ottawa.

DESAINVILLE, EDOUARD DE. 1984. Journey to the mouth of the Mackenzie River (1889-1894). Fram: The Journal of Polar Studies 1(2): 541-550.

FORD. JAMES. 1959. Eskimo Prehistory in the Vicinity of Point Barrow Alaska. Anthropological Papers of the American Museum of Natural History 47(1).

FRAKER, MARK AND JOHN BOCKSTOCE. 1980. Summer distribution of bowhead whales in the eastern Beaufort Sea. Marine Fisheries Review 42(9-10): 57-64.

FRANKLIN, JOHN. 1971. Narrative of a Second Expedition to the Shores of the Polar Sea in the Years 1825, 1826, and 1827. Hurtig: Edmonton.

GIDDINGS, J. LOUIS. 1952. The Arctic Woodland Culture of the Kobuk River. University of Pennsylvania, University Museum Monograph, 8.

GIDDINGS, J. LOUIS. 1964. The Archaeology of Cape Denbigh. Brown University Press: Providence, Rhode Island.

GODFREY, EARL. 1986. The Birds of Canada. National Museum of Natural Sciences: Ottawa.

GORDON, BRYAN. 1971. Salvage archaeology at Point Atkinson, Northwest Territories. MS 203, on file with the Archaeological Survey of Canada, Canadian Museum of Civilization, Ottawa. 76 pp.

GORDON, BRYAN. 1984. Selected bibliography of dental annular studies on various mammals. Zooarchaeological Research News, Supplement 2.

GRAYSON, DONALD. 1984. Quantitative Zooarchaeology: Topics in the Analysis of Archaeological Faunas. Academic Press: New York.

HALL, EDWIN. 1971. Kangiguksuk: a cultural reconstruction of a sixteenth century Eskimo site in northern Alaska. Arctic Anthropology 8(1): 1-101.

HARRISON, ALFRED. 1908. In Search of a Polar Continent, 1905-1908. E. Arnold: London.

HUDSON'S BAY COMPANY (HBC). Hudson's Bay Company Archives (microfilm copy), Public Archives of Canada, Ottawa.

JENNESS, DIAMOND. 1922. The Life of the Copper Eskimos. Report of the Canadian Arctic Expedition 1913-18 12(a).

JENNESS, DIAMOND. 1946. <u>Material Culture of the Copper Eskimo</u>. Report of the Canadian Arctic Expedition 1913-18 16.

JENNESS, DIAMOND. 1964. <u>Eskimo Administration: II. Canada</u>. Arctic Institute of North America, Technical Paper 14.

KARKLINS, KARL. 1985. <u>Glass Beads</u>. Parks Canada, Studies in Archaeology, Architecture and History.

KIDD, KENNETH AND MARTHA ANN KIDD. 1970. A Classification System for Glass Beads for the Use of Field Archaeologists. <u>Canadian Historic Sites: Occasional Papers in Archaeology and History</u> 1:46-89.

KLEIN, RICHARD AND KATHRYN CRUZ-URIBE. 1984. <u>The Analysis of Animal Bones from Archaeological Sites.</u> University of Chicago Press: Chicago.

KRECH, SHEPARD. 1979. Interethnic relations in the lower Mackenzie River region. <u>Arctic Anthropology</u> 16(2): 102-122.

LAVER, MARILYN and WILFRED BOKMAN. n.d. Analysis and X-radiography of ten iron fragments. MS 7034-4-2, on file with the Canadian Conservation Institute, Ottawa.

LEBLANC, RAYMOND. 1984. <u>The Rat Indian Creek Site and the Late Prehistoric Period in the Interior Northern Yukon.</u> National Museum of Man Mercury Series, Archaeological Survey of Canada Paper 120.

LEBLANC, RAYMOND. 1987. Report of Activities-NOGAP 1986: Northern Yukon to Cape Bathurst Peninsula. MS 2834, on file with the Archaeological Survey of Canada, Canadian Museum of Civilization, Ottawa.

LOWE, RONALD. 1984. <u>Siglit Inuvialuit Uqausiita Kipuktirutait: Basic Siglit Inuvialuit Eskimo Dictionary</u>. Committee for Original Peoples Entitlement: Inuvik, NWT.

LYMAN, R. LEE. 1984. Bone density and differential survivorship of fossil classes. Journal of Anthropological Archaeology 3: 259-299.

LYMAN, R. LEE. 1985. Bone frequencies: differential transport, in situ destruction, and the MGUI. Journal of Archaeological Science 12: 221-236.

M'CLURE, ROBERT. 1969. The Discovery of the North-West Passage, S. Osborn, ed. Hurtig: Edmonton.

MACFARLANE, RODERICK. 1891. On an expedition down the Begh-ula or Anderson River. The Canadian Record of Science, 4:28-53.

MACFARLANE, RODERICK. 1905. Notes on mammals collected and observed in the norther Mackenzie River District, Northwest Territories of Canada. Proceedings of the U.S. National Museum 28: 673-764.

MACKAY, ROSS. 1963. The Mackenzie Delta Area, N.W.T. Memoir of the Geographical Branch, Mines and Technical Surveys 8.

MACKENZIE, ALEXANDER. 1970. The Journals and Letters of Sir Alexander Mackenzie, W. Kaye Lamb, ed. Macmillan: Toronto.

MARTELL, A.M., D. DICKSINSON AND L. CASSELMAN. 1984. Wildlife of the Mackenzie Delta Region. Boreal institute for Northern Studies, Occasional Publication 15.

MATHIASSEN, THERKEL. 1927a. Archaeology of the Central Eskimos I. Report of the Fifth Thule Expedition 1921-24 4(1).

MATHIASSEN, THERKEL. 1927b. Archaeology of the Central Eskimos II. Report of the Fifth Thule Expedition 1921-24 4(2).

MATHIASSEN, THERKEL. 1930. Archaeological Collections from the Western Eskimos. Report of the Fifth Thule Expedition 1921-24 10(1).

MCCARTNEY, ALLEN AND JAMES SAVELLE. 1985. Thule Eskimo whaling in the central Canadian Arctic. Arctic Anthropology 22(2): 37-58.

MCGHEE, ROBERT. 1972. Copper Eskimo Prehistory. National Museum of Man, Publications in Archaeology 2.

MCGHEE, ROBERT. 1974. Beluga Hunters: An Archaeological Reconstruction of the History and Culture of the Mackenzie Delta Kittegaryumiut. Memorial University of Newfoundland, Newfoundland Social and Economic Studies 13.

MCGHEE, ROBERT. 1986. The Mackenzie Inuit: historical and ethnographic background. Paper presented to the Annual Meeting of the Canadian Archaeological Association, Toronto.

MIERTSCHING, JOHANN. 1967. Frozen Ships: The Arctic Diary of Johann Miertsching, L. H. Neatby, trans. Macmillan: Toronto.

MILLER, FRANK. 1974. Biology of the Kaminuriak population of barren-ground caribou, Part 2. Canadian Wildlife Service Report Series 31.

MORLAN, RICHARD. 1972. The Cadzow Lake Site (MjVi-1): a multi-component historic Kutchin camp. National Museum of Man, Mercury Series, Archaeological Survey of Canada Paper 3.

MORRISON, DAVID. 1981. A preliminary statement on Neo-Eskimo occupations in western Coronation Gulf, N.W.T. Arctic 34(3): 261-269.

MORRISON, DAVID. 1983a. Thule Culture in Western Coronation Gulf, N.W.T. National Museum of Man, Mercury Series, Archaeological Survey of Canada Paper 116.

MORRISON, DAVID. 1983b. Thule sea mammal hunting in the western central Arctic. Arctic Anthropology 20(2): 61-78.

MORRISON, DAVID. 1984. A note on Thule culture dogs from Coronation Gulf, N.W.T. <u>Canadian Journal of Archaeology</u> 8(2): 149–157.

MORRISON, DAVID. in press. Inuit and Kutchin bone and antler industries in northwestern Canada. <u>Canadian Journal of Archaeology</u>.

MURDOCH, JOHN. 1892. <u>Ethnological Results of the Point Barrow Expedition.</u> Ninth Annual Report of the Bureau of American Ethnology 1887–88.

NELSON, EDWARD WILLIAM. 1983 (orig. 1899). <u>The Eskimo About Bering Strait.</u> Smithsonian Institution Press: Washington.

NULIGAK. 1966. <u>I, Nuligak,</u> Maurice Metayer, trans. Peter Martin: Toronto.

PETITOT, EMILE. 1970. <u>The Amerindians of the Canadian Northwest in the 19th Century, as seen by Emile Petitot, Volume 1: The Tchiglit Eskimos,</u> Donat Savoie, ed. Mackenzie Delta Research Project 9.

PETITOT, EMILE. 1981. <u>Among the Chiglit Eskimos,</u> Otto Hahn, trans. Institute for Northern Studies, Occasional Publication 10.

PRESLEY, STERLING. 1984. Determination of Site Seasonality, Using Tooth Annuli Technique. MS 2294, on file with the Archaeological Survey of Canada, Canadian Museum of Civilization, Ottawa.

PULLEN, H.F. 1979. <u>The Pullen Expedition.</u> Arctic History Press: Toronto.

RICHARDSON, JOHN. 1851. <u>Arctic Searching Expedition,</u> vol. 1. Longmans, Brown, Green, and Longmans: London.

RICK, ANNE. 1980. Non-cetacean vertebrate remains from two Thule winter houses on Somerset Island, N.W.T. <u>Canadian Journal of Archaeology</u> 4: 99–117.

RUSSELL, FRANK. 1898. <u>Explorations in the Far North.</u> University of Iowa
Press: DesMoines.

SIEGEL, SIDNEY. 1956. <u>Nonparametric Statistics.</u> McGraw-Hill: New York.

SIMPSON, THOMAS. 1843. <u>Narrative of the Discoveries on the North Coast
of America.</u> R. Bentley: London.

SMITH, DEREK. 1984. Mackenzie Delta Eskimo. In, <u>Handbook of North
American Indians, Volume 5: Arctic</u>, D. Damas, ed., pp. 347-358. Smithsonian
Institution: Washington.

SPEISS, ARTHUR. 1979. <u>Reindeer and Caribou Hunters.</u> Academic Press: New
York.

SPENCER, ROBERT. 1959. <u>The North Alaskan Eskimo: a Study in Ecology and
Society.</u> Bureau of American Ethnology Bulletin 171.

SPETH, JOHN. 1983. <u>Bison Kills and Bone Counts: Decision Making by
Ancient Hunters.</u> University of Chicago Press: Chicago.

STAGER, JOHN. 1967. Fort Anderson. <u>Geographical Bulletin</u> 9(1): 45-56.

STEFANSSON, VILHJALMUR. 1913. The distribution of human and animal life
in western Arctic America. <u>The Geographical Journal</u> 41(5): 449-460.

STEFANSSON, VILHJALMUR. 1914. <u>The Stefansson-Anderson Arctic
Expedition: Preliminary Ethnological Results.</u> Anthropological Papers of the
American Museum of Natural History 14(1).

STEFANSSON, VILHMALMUR. 1922. <u>Hunters of the Great North.</u> Harcourt,
Brace: New York.

STEFANSSON, VILHJALMUR. 1962 (orig. 1913). <u>My Life with the Eskimo.</u>
Collier: New York.

STROMBERG, RICHARD. 1987. Cache Point (NhTs-2) and Mackenzie Inuit prehistory. Paper presented to the Annual Meeting of the Society for American Archaeology, Toronto.

UNGLIK, HENRY. 1978. Metallurgical Examination of a Tin Can of British Origin from Devon Island in the Arctic. MS, on file with the National Historic Parks and Sites Branch, Parks Canada, Ottawa. 42 pp.

USHER, PETER. 1971. The Canadian Western Arctic: a century of change. Anthropologica, n.s. 13(1-2): 169-183.

WENTZEL, W.F. 1823. Notice of the attempts to reach the sea by Mackenzie's River. Edinburgh Philosophical Journal 8: 78-9.

WHITE, THEODORE. 1953. A method of calculating the dietary percentage of various food animals utilized by aboriginal peoples. American Antiquity 19: 396-398.

WHITTAKER, C.E. 1937. Arctic Eskimo. Seeley, Service and Co.: London.

YORGA, BRIAN. 1979. Washout: A Western Thule Site on Herschel Island, Yukon Territory. National Museum of Man, Mercury Series, Archaeological Survey of Canada Paper 98.

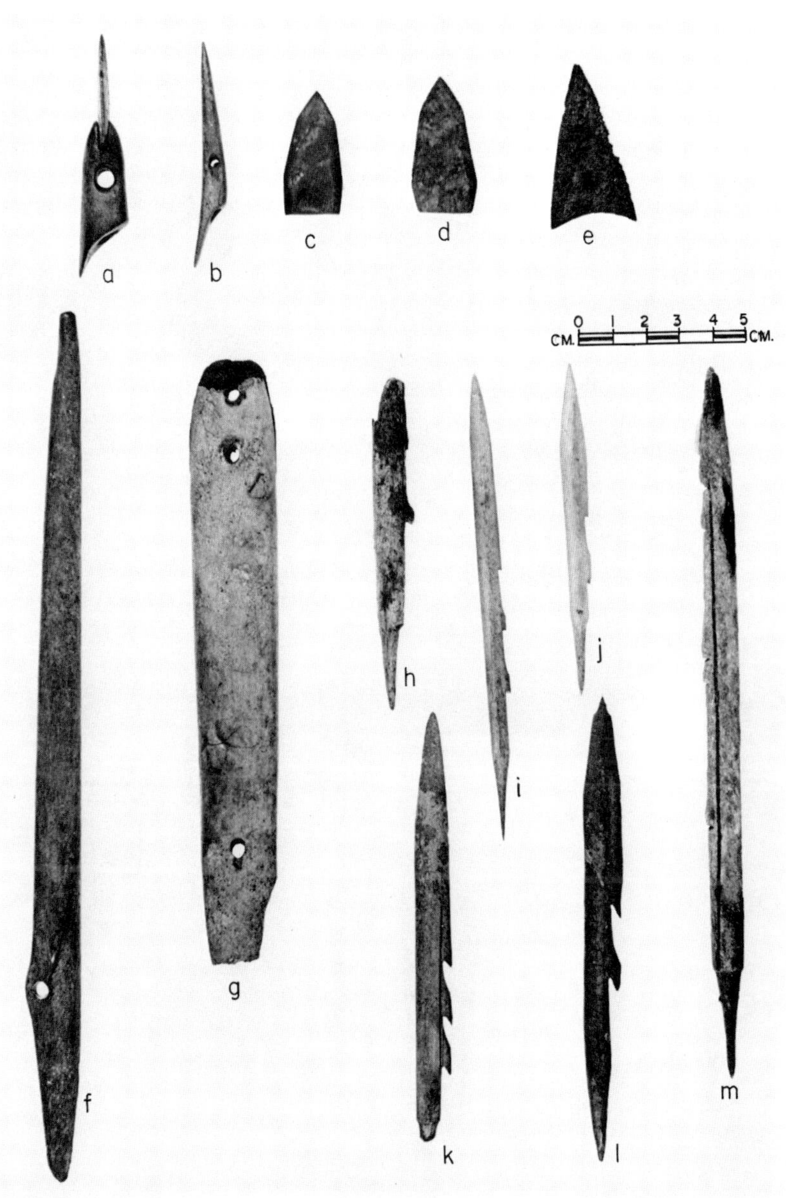

HUNTING GEAR

PLATE 2

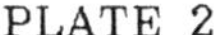

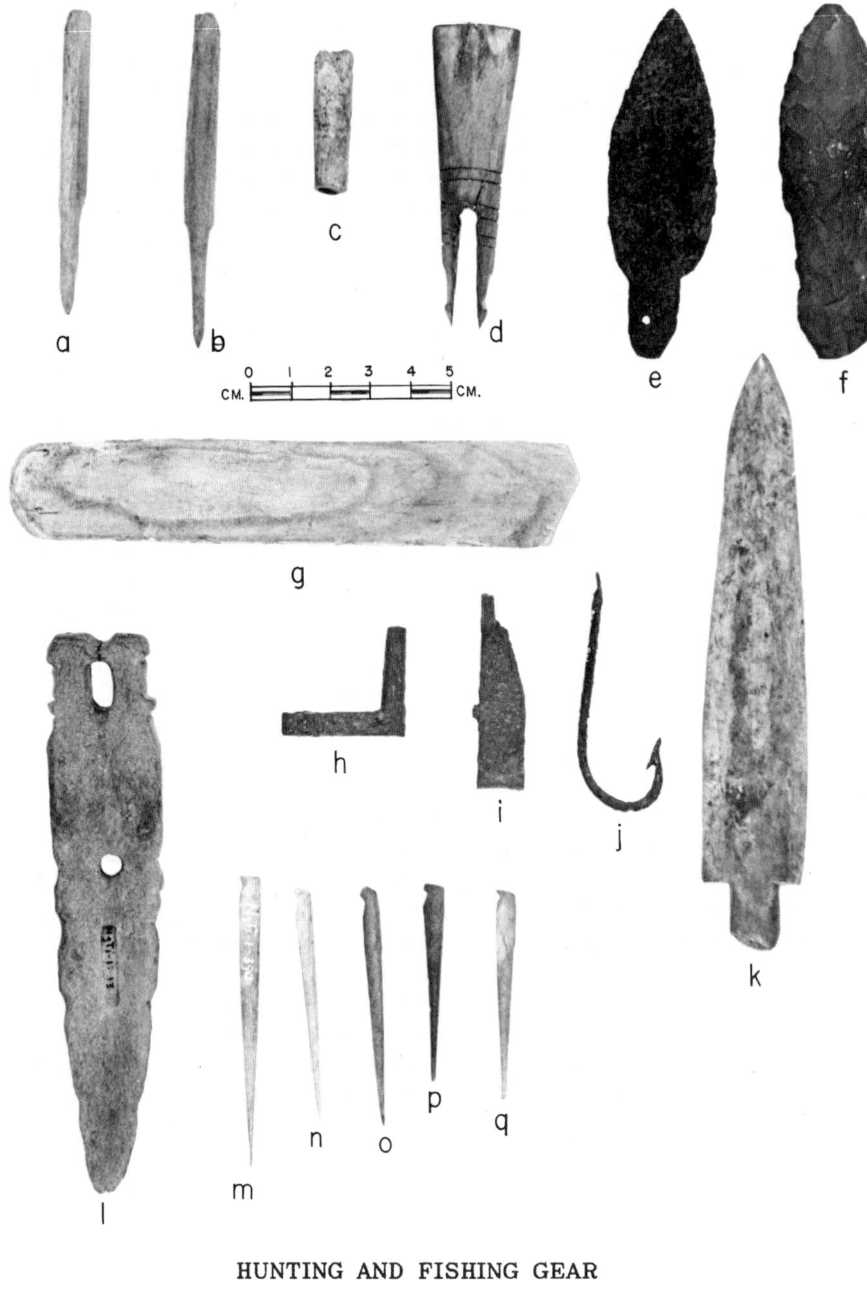

HUNTING AND FISHING GEAR

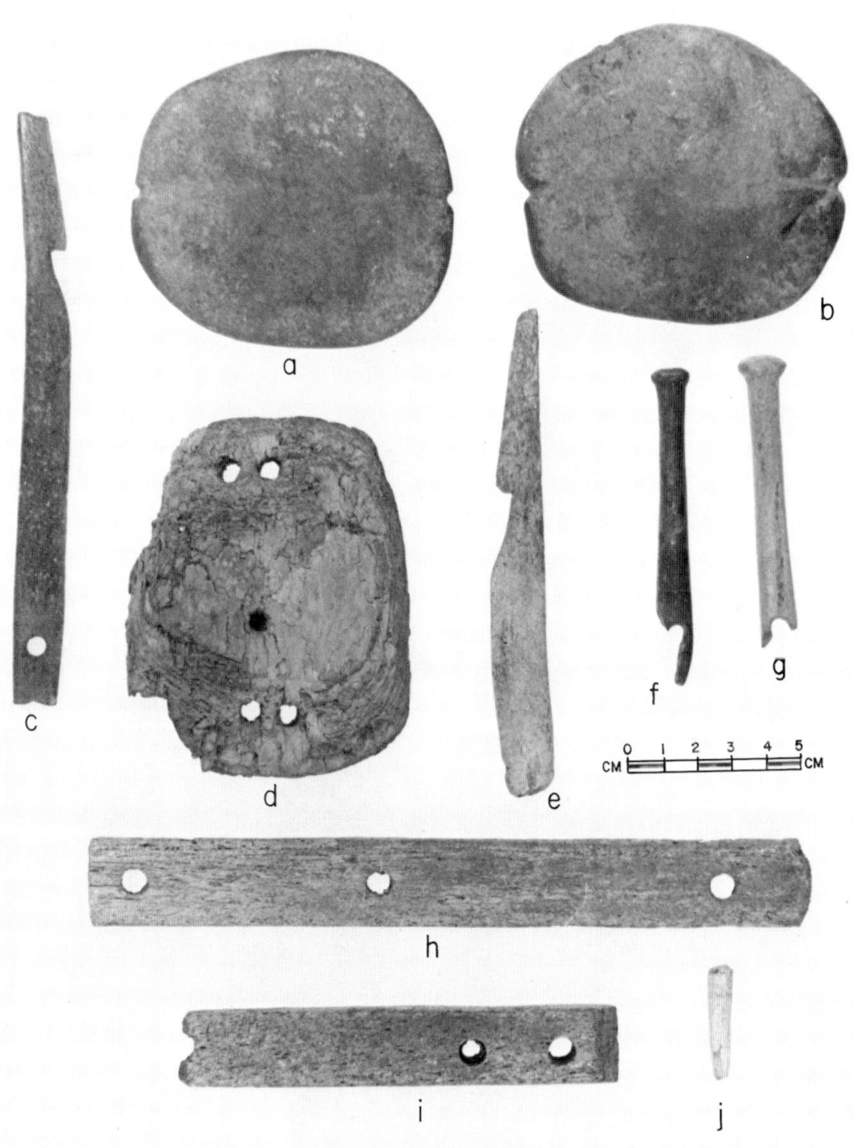

FISHING AND TRANSPORTATION GEAR

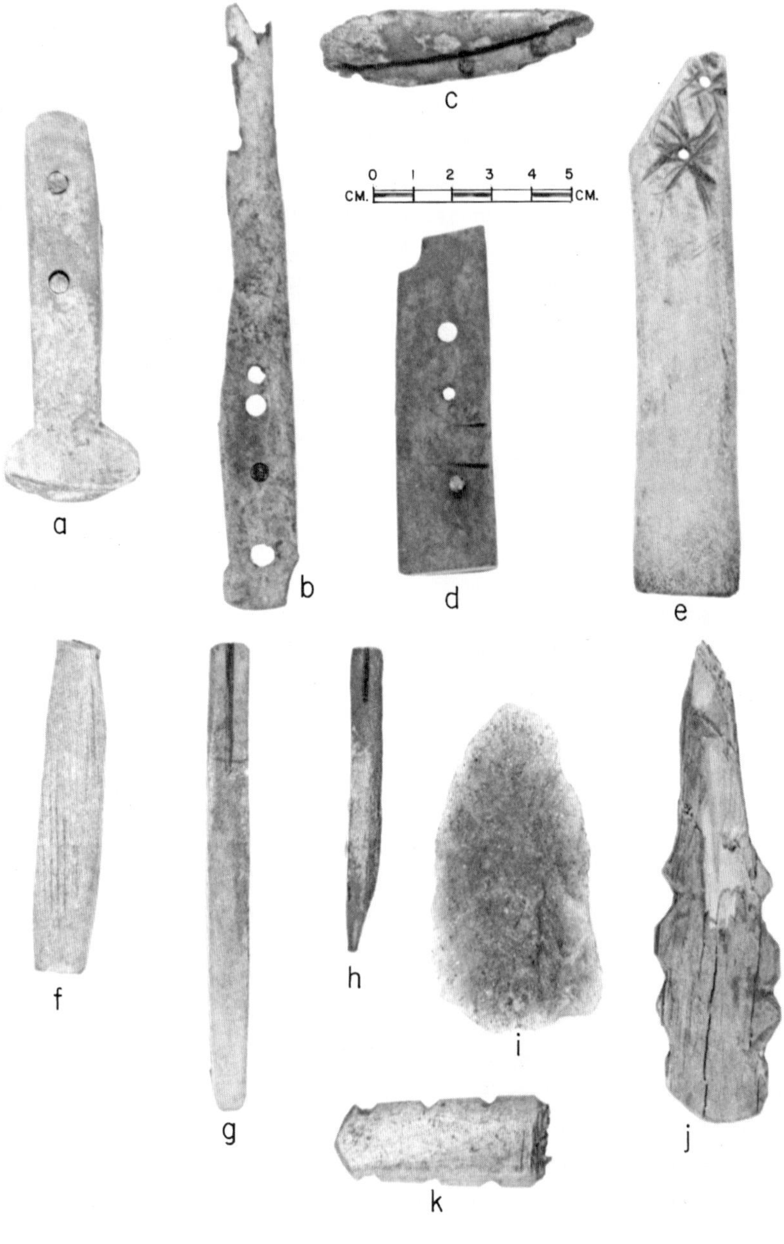

MEN'S TOOLS

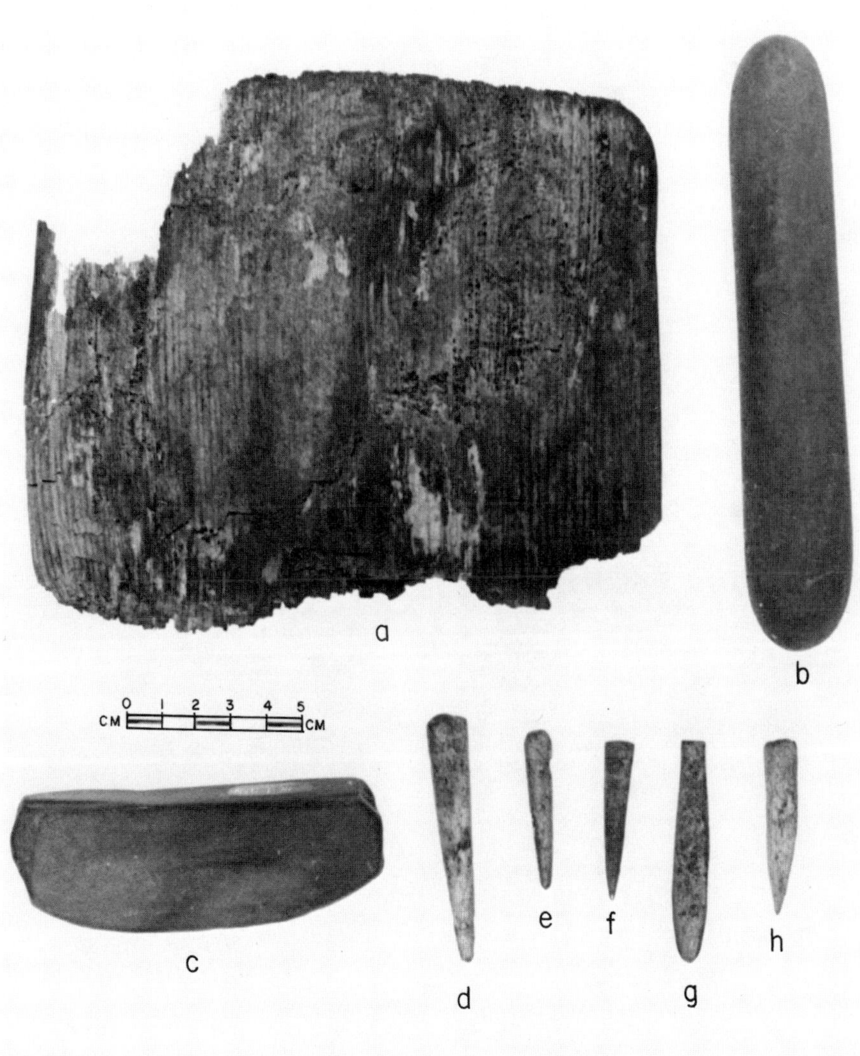

MEN'S TOOLS

PLATE 6

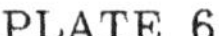

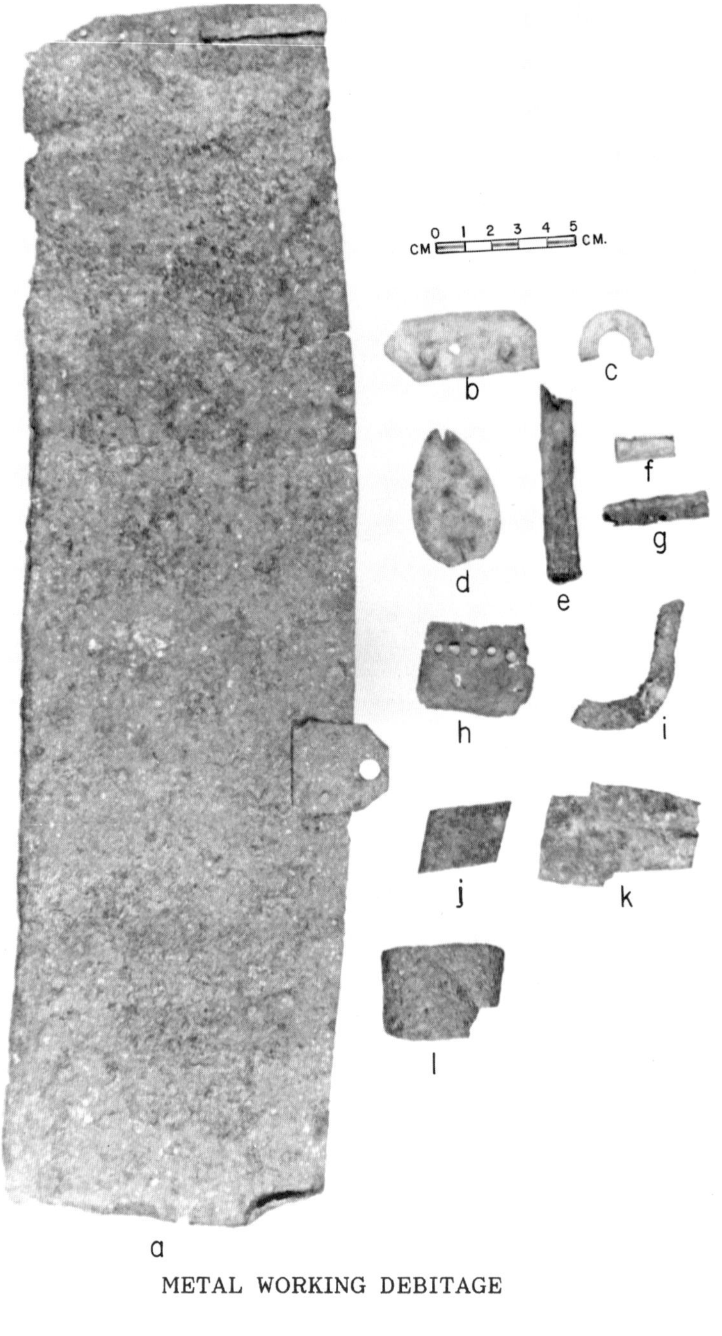

METAL WORKING DEBITAGE

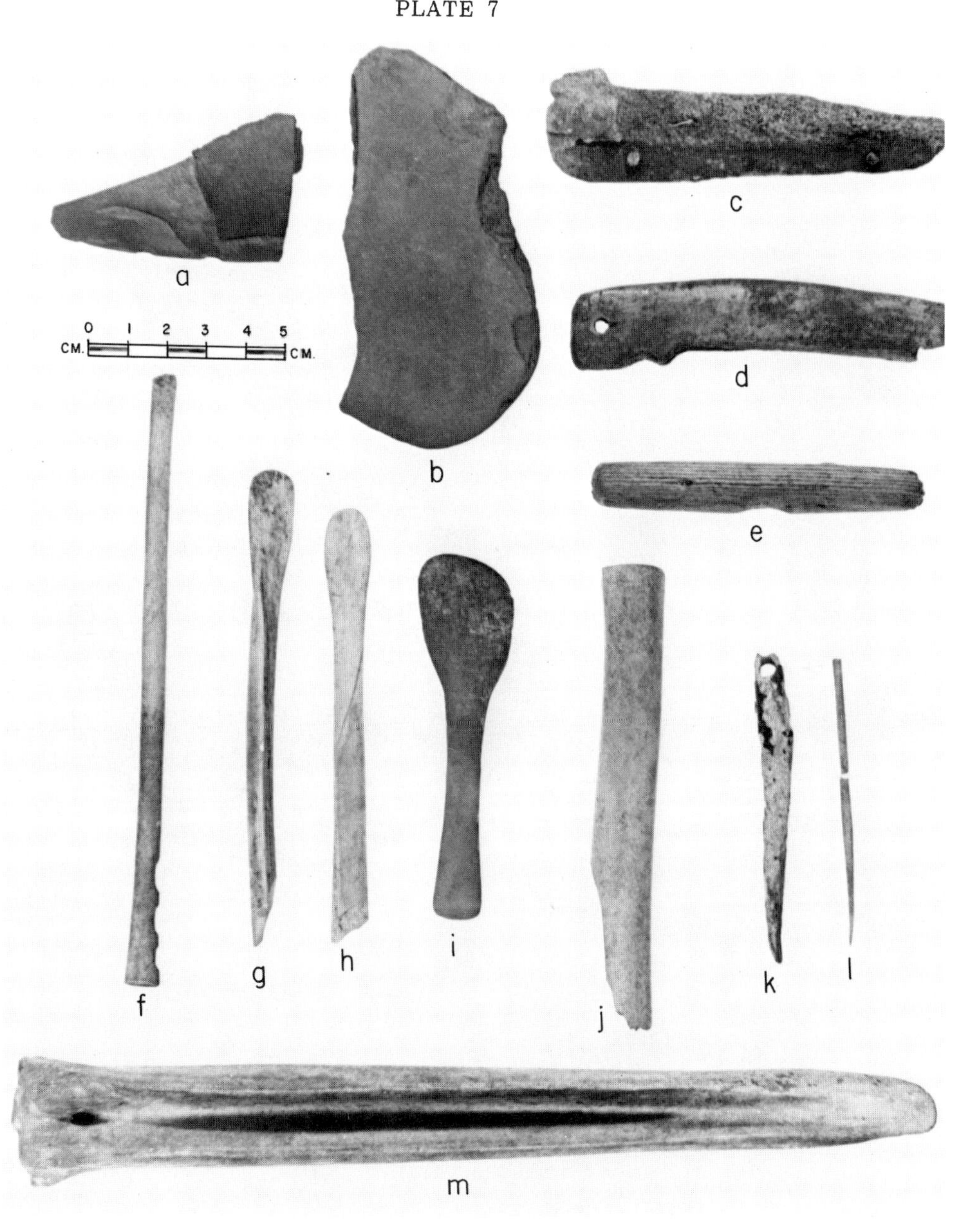

WOMEN'S TOOLS AND DOMESTIC ITEMS

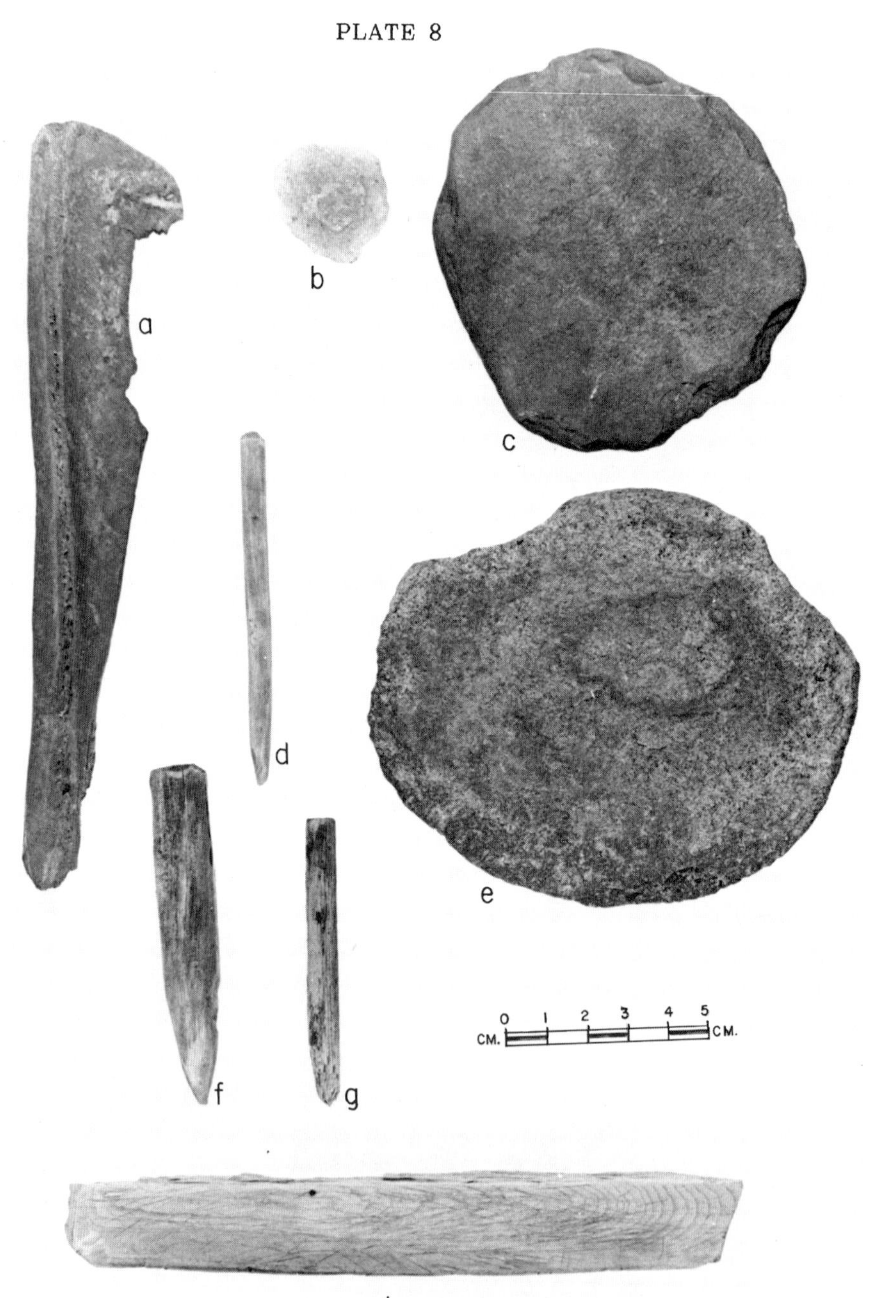

WOMEN'S TOOLS AND DOMESTIC ITEMS

POTTERY AND SOAPSTONE VESSEL FRAGMENTS

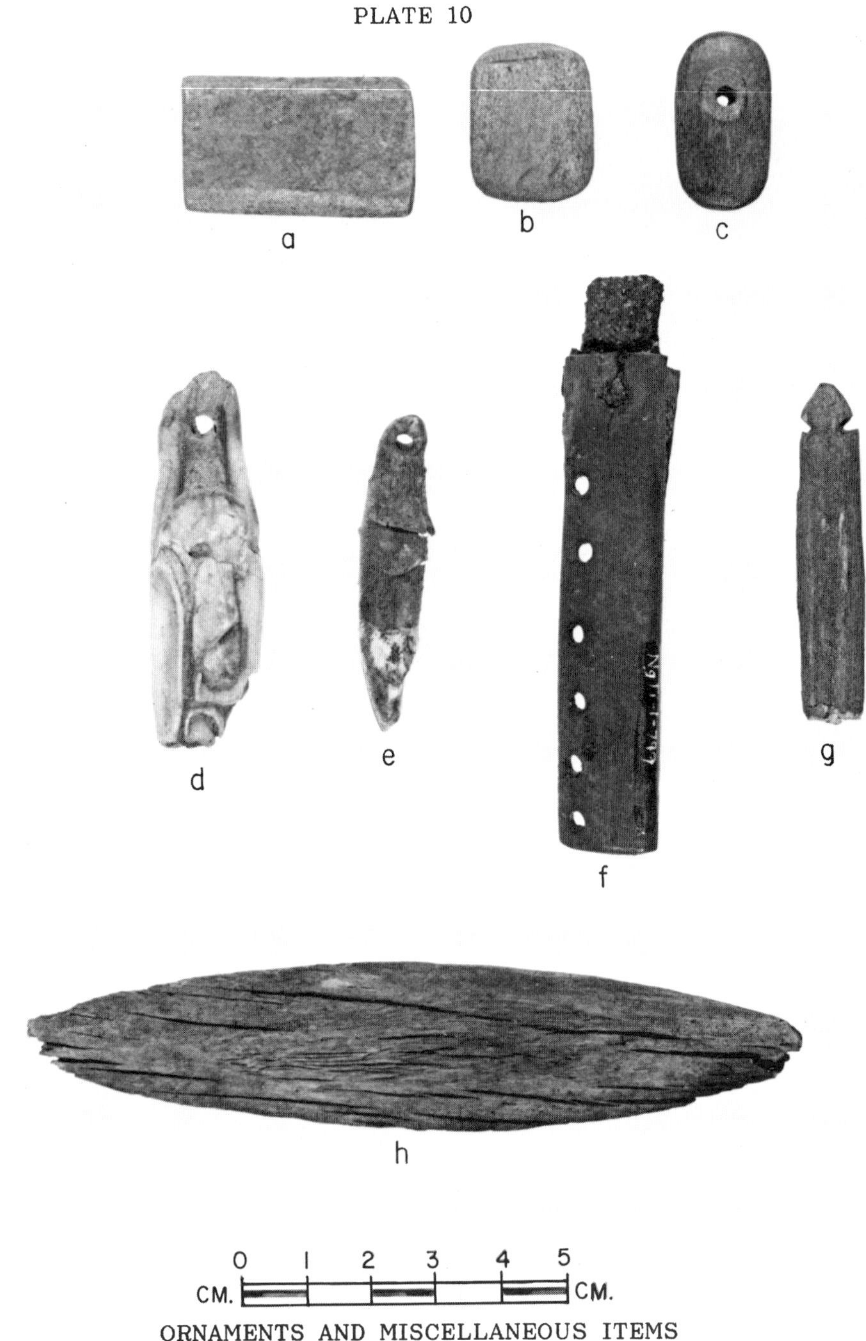

ORNAMENTS AND MISCELLANEOUS ITEMS